Text and Texture

Text and Texture

Close Readings of Selected Biblical Texts

a.

Michael Fishbane

Schocken Books • New York

First published by Schocken Books 1979
10 9 8 7 6 5 4 3 2 1   79 80 81 82

Copyright © 1979 by Schocken Books Inc.

Library of Congress Cataloging in Publication Data

Fishbane, Michael A
    Text and texture.

    Includes index.
    1. Bible.   O.T.—Criticism, interpretation, etc.
    I.   Title.
    BS1171.2.F57   221.6   79-14083

Manufactured in the United States of America

FOR MONA

"you are my flower"

Contents

Preface

This book was written with several interrelated objectives in mind. I wanted to extend the contours of biblical literacy to persons not otherwise engaged in Bible study, and to teach a properly literary reading of the biblical text. Such a reading, I believe, may serve to bring the modern reader to a confrontation with the deepest levels of literary and religious coherence in the Bible. Thus, while scholars will easily recognize my departure from conventional approaches to and interpretations of familiar texts, I have not sought to advocate my positions against those of others. To the contrary—I have tried to allow the reader to engage the texts studied through my particular interpretations of them, not through the tangled history of exegesis. I have, of course, learned from many direct and indirect teachers, and have tried to acknowledge these debts in the notes. But the reader interested in fuller bibliographies and cross-references will have to go elsewhere. These notes are ultimately secondary to my text, just as my interpretations are secondary to the biblical text itself. It is a new encounter with the words of this text that I have sought to sponsor. All translations found herein are my own.

In the birth of a book there are many midwives. Let me first thank Lily Edelman who, many years ago, as then director of the B'nai B'rith Adult Education Commission, invited me to write a book of literary interpretations of biblical texts. Her continuous interest in my work, even after she was no longer directly involved, is gratefully acknowledged. The present book is the final harvest of that invitation. Then there are my many Brandeis students who, particularly in the mid-seventies and in my 'NEJS 96' course, provided the occasion and responsive setting for many ideas then struggling for proper formulation. I thank them all, especially those who became, in time, more friends than students. As my ideas took on literary shape, many colleagues and friends graciously responded to my work. I therefore wish to thank Nahum Glatzer, Allen Grossman, Nahum Sarna, George Savran, and Larry Weinstein for their attentive and helpful observations on early drafts.

In other matters, Jack Goldstein, Dean of Faculty at Brandeis University, generously made available funds to defray typing expenses incurred in connection with preparing the manuscript. Geza Vermes, editor of the *Journal of Jewish Studies*, kindly consented to my reuse of materials originally appearing in volume 26 (1975), pages 15-38. And Ann Leonard, my typist, deserves special thanks for her cheerful and prompt professional work. Finally, I am most deeply appreciative to Seymour Barofsky, Patricia Woodruff, and the staff at Schocken Books for their courtesy, care, and efficiency in all matters pertaining to the production of this book. I am honored to be associated with the Schocken Books tradition.

This Preface would be far from complete until I thank you, Mona, for your intimate involvement with the ideas and formulations of this book at every stage of its development. You have understood the thoughts of my soul before they found speech, and have nurtured their birth. As my life partner, you are my constant blessing. This book is dedicated to you.

Michael Fishbane

Introduction

There are several interrelated considerations regarding the study of the Hebrew Bible which underpin the texts analyzed in this book. My realization of them has shaped my orientation to Scripture.

The first point I wish to stress is that the Bible is a religious teaching, recording moments of meeting between God and man, and, more particularly, the ongoing relationship between the Unconditioned One and the people of Israel. The creature before, in search of, and in response to his creator; the creator before, in search of, and in response to His creatures: these are the eternal subjects of the Bible. The dialectic of response and responsibility between the divine Presence and the religious spirit of man covers all areas of life. Nothing is excluded or excludable.

The received text of Scripture is, as Plato would say, the rescued speech of these meetings.[1] Each "rescued" event is expressed by a dense blend of a particular historical moment and inherited or spontaneous style. Form is inseparable from content, such that every textual formulation of an event constructs a unique literary reality; to imagine a different formulation of it would be to construct a different reality. It is in this fundamental sense, at least, that the Bible is to be understood as revelation. Through its words, the world of a text, and the multiple worlds of its many texts, are disclosed.[2]

This leads to a second matter. As a literary artifact, the words of the Bible require an interpreter for renewed life. Indeed, reading rehearses the latent meanings of a text: meaning unfolds in the process of reading, it being a function of the dialectic which takes place between a particular reader and a particular text. For example, terse narrative descriptions—such as characterize the books of Genesis, Judges, and Samuel—may stimulate a reader to actively supplement underdeveloped details. These participant assumptions build up in a reader's mind and affect his evaluations of the unfolding narrative.[3] Of course, new narrative disclosures may complement earlier estimations, require their revision, or otherwise add to the density of meanings which accumulate in the course of reading. But this phenomenon does not depreciate the fundamental reciprocity between text and reader at work; it rather confirms it. Thus an interpreter is dependent upon the text given to his inspection, even as the text is dependent upon him. For it is the reader who performs the text in his mind, lingers in its silences and suggestions, and so serves as its midwife and voice.

Helping to mediate between the words of the biblical text and its dependence upon a reader for meaning are several stylistic conventions. One particularly recurrent and transparent technique is the theme-word. Because Hebrew words are essentially built around triliteral stems, the same stem may recur in one and the same text in different nominal, verbal, and adjectival forms. Such repetition, where it occurs, gives a text special texture; and it also serves to highlight major and minor features of content. A reader may thus be guided or provoked towards certain interpretations on the basis of theme-words recurrent in one or several texts which are thereby brought into association. And what applies to words is equally pertinent with respect to larger themes or motifs. Through such stylistic means, latent networks of intra- and intertextual meaning may be perceived by an interpreter.

The stylistic structuring of literary texts is another compositional convention particularly common in the Bible, and affects the formation of single texts and larger literary cycles. Because the Bible is a national anthology of diverse genres produced over many centuries, its texts reflect not only the creative impulse of their original composers, but that of its revisers and arrangers as well. An individual unit may be structured according to a symmetrical or other arrangement of its words and themes; or its compositional form may be affected by new material subsequently worked into the original contents. As smaller units are joined to comprise larger literary blocks, which may themselves be structured according to one scheme or another, a purely compositional technique shades into an editorial one. More sustained narrative unities are thus formed, reflecting increasingly more complex literary and cultural processes.

Perception of the stylistic and editorial arrangement of literary materials may thus bear on one's appreciation of both the modulation of textual sequences and the simultaneity of meanings which comprise biblical texts. For it must be stressed that stylistic conventions allow the voice of a text to speak on its own terms and according to its own arrangement. The more conscious a reader is of these conventions, the less likely will he be to subjectivize a text irresponsibly; the more likely will his reading tend towards a disciplined freedom: spontaneity within necessity.

In addition to such internal textual features as have just been briefly outlined, a reader must also be attentive to external, comparative issues. Because the preserved biblical texts are but fragments of a larger cultural enterprise, the interpreter must be familiar with the contemporaneous ancient Near Eastern literatures and cultures. What may be obscurely instanced in the Bible is often fully attested beyond it. Comparisons can be illuminating. But they should always be a means and not an end for the biblical interpreter, whose task is to understand the Bible's unique—and ultimately self-referential—literary realities.

A final consideration may be mentioned. While the trend of my previous remarks has been to stress the givenness of biblical texts as rescued responses to the initiating presence and mystery of God in the course of human life, there is a fundamental sense in which these texts also testify to their inherent limitations, and so provide the means whereby they may be transcended. The diversity of historical and personal expressions found in the Bible on any number of issues—like wonder, hope or suffering—indicates the deep need of the persons and generations of biblical Israel to speak to and of God in their own terms. Indeed, it is precisely this ensemble of voices which shows each particular formulation to be but one humanized expression of the religious imagination. So seen, biblical texts are fundamentally pointers to the image of God by man, and projections of the images of man on God. Accordingly, these images must not become verbal icons, no matter how rich the individual pattern of meanings which they may sponser.

When the Bible will be so appreciated for preserving historical examples of religious responses to God as well as diverse modes of being in God's world, its texts will not stand between man and God; they will rather bring us—the readers —beyond its literary formulations and to the nameless and Unconditioned One, the Lord of life and death. Thoughts similar to these, I believe, led Martin Buber to speak the following words more than half a century ago:

The reader of the Bible must attempt to understand it not as a work of literature but as the basic documentation of the unconditional's effect on the spirit of the Jewish people; whatever his knowledge of old as well as new exegesis, he will search beyond it for the original meaning of each passage. No matter how familiar he is with modern biblical criticism's distinction between sources, he will penetrate beyond this criticism to more profound distinctions and connections.... He will read the Bible with an appreciation of its poetic form, but also with an intuitive grasp of the suprapoetic element which transcends all form. To such a reader the Bible will reveal a hidden treasure and the operation of primal forces from which the seed of a new religiosity can derive sustenance and substance.[4]

A few observations may now be provided about the texts gathered here for study. Each of the three sections of the table of contents is dedicated to a different type of text. The first part deals with narrative texts, considered both as independent entities and as units within larger literary cycles; the second part takes texts of direct speech as its subject, and so deals with a sermon and several types of prayers; and the third part takes up a theme and a motif which recur throughout the Bible, and considers their diverse historical expressions and applications. Within this overall framework, textual styles and structures will be considered; types of literary and theological unity will be considered; and religious thoughts and expressions will be discussed. An intentional thematic emphasis, however, gives this diverse collection of literary styles and religious topics some coherence. Such issues as the creation, the sacred space of Eden, the exodus, prophetic destiny, and prayer are treated in more than one, and usually in all three parts. Perhaps this recurrence will further enable the reader to perceive some of the dynamic unities within diversities which help constitute the Hebrew Bible.

Narratives and Narrative Cycles

1. Genesis 1:1-2:4a /
The Creation

The mind of man has always been fascinated by the mysteries of origins. Tales and texts of every sort and from every civilization attest to a basic curiosity about the origins of the things of the world, their interconnections and hierarchies, and their relations to the origin of the created world itself. Such knowledge provides cognitive control over the mysteries of beginnings which haunt human consciousness. The sacred telling of origins, or *mythos*, discloses the ordering of life at creation.[1]

As with other texts of origins, Genesis 1:1-2:4a is a product of language in its creative vitality. Man must surely have intuited and experienced very early the magical power of words to create reality and control imagination. What is sayable is knowable. And what can be said can be shared and transmitted. To give verbal shape to experience is to control the understanding of it indefinitely. Language both constructs a universe of meaning and becomes the means whereby that universe is presented to consciousness.

The nineteenth-century philosopher of language Wilhelm von Humbolt clarified this power of language to narrate mysteries and tell origins. "At the same time that language has a character that is indeed internal," he noted, "it also exists as an independent and external fact which exerts constraint on man."[2] By this remark von Humbolt emphasized that language shapes reality. In giving a form to man's insight that can be retained, language restricts him, too. It freezes his vision of one moment and holds him to it. What it gives with one hand it takes away with the other. The broad diversity of biblical and ancient Near Eastern creation-texts now extant suggests these other introductory points:

1. Within any particular culture a variety of creation accounts—often mutually exclusive—may coexist. Each particular version makes an independent assertion about the nature of being and becoming and each one appears exclusively as "the Creation."

2. These multiple stories of creation arise out of concrete historical situations and have specific purposes, be they to laud

a particular god or give value to specific places and institutions. Accordingly, different creation texts in any one culture justify different institutions or theological orientations.³ A sacred telling is always saturated with the values and concerns of a particular culture at a particular time. While each creation account makes a universal claim, it is necessarily a product of its particular cultural or religious orientation.

3. Any sacred telling, or *mythos*, transcends its parts and is a total teaching. A *mythos* must never be reduced to a discursive summary of its contents or purposes. Its power is presented through the total interaction of its images, sequences, and values. And it teaches by the way it accounts for the mystery of origins, by the unique way it fills the void of mystery with imagination.

In the actual text of Genesis 1:1–2:4a, presented below, a world is "worded forth":

> At the beginning of Elohim's creation of heaven and earth,
> The earth was formless and void,
> Darkness was on the face of the deep,
> And the Wind of Elohim swirled on the face of the waters.
>
> Elohim said:
> "Let there be light!"
> And light was there.
> Elohim saw that the light was good.
> Then Elohim separated the light from the darkness.
> Elohim called the light: "Day!" and He called the darkness: "Night!"
>
> There was setting; there was dawning; day one.
>
> Elohim said:
> "Let there be firmament betwixt the waters,
> That it separate between water and water!"
> Elohim made the firmament and separated between
> The waters beneath the firmament and the waters above the firmament.
> And it was so.
> Then Elohim called the firmament: "Heaven!"
>
> There was setting; there was dawning; a second day.
>
> Elohim said:
> "Let the waters under the heavens be gathered in one place
> That the dry land be seen!"
> And it was so.
> Then Elohim called the dry land: "Earth!"

And the gathered waters He called: "Sea!"
Elohim saw that it was good.

Elohim said:
"Let the earth grow grass, seed-shooting plants, fruit trees giving
Fruit of their kind, whose seed is in it on the earth!"
And it was so.

And the earth gave grass, seed-shooting plants of its kind, and
Trees giving fruit of their kind, whose seed is in it.
Elohim saw that it was good.

There was setting; there was dawning; a third day.

Elohim said:
"Let there be lights in the firmament of the heaven to separate
Between the day and the night, that they be as signs
And stations and days and years, and that they be
As lights in the firmament of the heaven to light up the earth!"
And it was so.
Elohim made the two great lights: the great light
For the dominion of the day, and the lesser light
For the dominion of the night, and the stars.
Elohim put them in the firmament of the heaven to light up the
    earth,
To have dominion during the day and the night,
And to separate between the light and the darkness.
Elohim saw that it was good.

There was setting; there was dawning; a fourth day.

Elohim said:
"Let the waters swarm with a swarm of living beings, and
Winged birds winging over the earth against the
Face of the firmament of the heaven!"
Elohim created the great sea-dragons and every
Living, stirring being with which the waters swarm, of their
    kind,
And every winged bird of its kind.
Elohim saw that it was good.
Then Elohim blessed them saying:
"Be fruitful and multiply and fill the waters of the sea,
And let the birds multiply on the earth."

There was setting; there was dawning; a fifth day.

Elohim said:
"Let the earth give living beings of its kind:
Cattle and reptiles and wild animals of each kind!"
And it was so.
Thus Elohim made the wild animals of each kind,

Cattle of each kind, and every land reptile of each kind!"
Elohim saw that it was good.
Elohim said:
"Let us make Man in our image and our visage, that they
Rule over the fish of the sea, the birds of the sky, the herd
Animals and the whole earth, and every reptile which stirs on
    the earth!"

Elohim created the Man in his image;
He created him in the image of Elohim;
He created them male and female.
And Elohim blessed them, and Elohim said to them:
"Be fruitful and multiply and fill the earth and subdue it;
And rule over the fish of the sea, the birds of the sky,
And every being which stirs on the earth!"
And Elohim said
"Indeed! I have given you all the seed-shooting plants which are
On the face of the earth; and I have given you every
Seed-sending fruit tree for food; and for every being of the
    earth,
Every bird of the sky and every reptile of the earth
Which has a living spirit,
All green plants for eating."
And it was so.
Elohim saw everything that He did
And it was very good.

There was setting; there was dawning: the sixth day.

The heaven and earth were finished,
And everything therein;
Elohim finished His work on the Seventh Day
And rested from His work on the Seventh Day.
Elohim blessed the Seventh Day.
And set it apart;
For on that Day Elohim rested from all His work of creation.

This is the account of the heaven and the earth, at the time of their
    creation.

The preceding narrative does not speak of origins and creations that occurred "once upon a time," but of *the* Creation that occurred "Once, at the beginning of time." This prologue takes the reader out of his own time and into the primordial time that precedes all human and cultural experience. Indeed, it so effectively transports him into the temporal-literary framework of the text that any question as to just how the narrator could know what occurred "at the beginning" is raised only belatedly. Only after the reading experience does the reader sense that perhaps this text is but a literary-theological response to the mystery of origins.

Both the reading experience of Genesis 1:1–2:4*a* and its content, its silences and speeches, are controlled by the narrator: the breaking of the initial, primordial silence by speech ("At the beginning"); the interruptions or linkages of the various speeches by silences; the closing of the text in its entirety into the silence of completed action. The narrator also determines the fundamental framework of the text, from the initial, forward-looking "At the beginning of Elohim's creation of heaven and earth," to the concluding and reflective "This is the account of the heaven and the earth, at the time of their creation."

The narrator, moreover, fills in the spaces between the various speeches of God. He provides both introductions to God's words ("Elohim said") and reports of the divine attitude ("And Elohim saw that it was good"). He reports the acts of creation ("Elohim said: Let there be...," "There was," "Elohim created," or "And it was so") and provides the transitions from day to day ("There was setting; there was dawning...").

The voice of the narrator is indeed a dominating presence, disclosing background, introducing action, summarizing action, and providing for continuity. But in another sense the narrator's presence is more modest, merely providing the narrative thread which laces the speeches of Elohim. While the words of the narrator are creative in the sense that they shape the literary form and style of this text, the words of God are creative in a more fundamental sense. God's speaking and creating are one and indissoluble. His words create and order the heaven and the earth; they give a syntax to the formless and the void, they transform the primordial, undifferentiated unity into order and classification.[4]

The prosaic, reflective discourse of the human speaker ("there was") counterpoints the commanding tones ("Let there be") of the divine speeches, as well as the force expressed in naming the things of creation ("Day!" "Heaven!" "Earth!"). Indeed, the speeches of Elohim would be overpowering without the calming and alternating rhythm of the human speeches which precede, intervene between, and follow them.

It is precisely through this divine–human counterpoint that two dramatic aspects of Genesis 1:1–2:4*a* emerge. First is the action-result sequence whereby the daily "creations" are brought into existence by speeches of action ("Let there be") and of result ("And there was"). The second aspect consists of the almost stereotyped repetition of key words (e.g., "created," "saw," "separated," "good"), which allows the reader to focus fully on the uniqueness of each day and its events. The concluding daily refrain ("There was setting; there was dawning: day x") at once sums up what has passed and anticipates what is to follow.

The text thus provides a reflection of an orderly, harmonious creation. The alternation of the narrator's voice with divine speech, of description with prescription, serves to present "the creation" as a dispassionate recitation recurrently punctuated with vital divine energy. The text shifts rhythmically between actions and results which utilize the same words ("separate" ..."call"..."see"..."make") and sequences. Its economy of vocabulary and technique produces a dictum of controlled energy and force.

No easy separation can be made between the style and meaning of the text. Both are involved, and any attempt to introduce a dichotomy between them, to distinguish between "objective" facts of form and subjective interpretations of meaning, is singularly misguided. The text's meaning is uniquely a function of the active interchange between the reader and what the text continuously evokes in him by virtue of its perceived form and style.

With respect to Genesis 1:1-2:4a, the formality of its sequences, the repetition of its key words, and the serialization of its contents combine to produce several theological meanings: that Elohim, alone, "at the beginning," created a good, ordered world; that He "separated" and hierarchically ordered the primordial mass into a "good" pattern; that the created world of nature is, as a result, a harmony; and that Elohim is Omnipotent and without rival.

Moreover, the structure of the text resembles a pyramid: each succeeding day is accorded more space than its predecessor. The events of the second day are presented more expansively than those of the first, the third more than the second, the fourth more than the third...and the sixth most of all. The whole configuration, in fact, moves towards this climactic day; a day distinguished by the creation of mankind, a day set apart as "very good" (all the others were simply "good"), and a day in which the divine beings of the pantheon are involved in the creation (note the phrase: "Let *us*";[5] the other creations are invoked by God). A day with special determination, it is called "*the* sixth day" (all other days are referred to indeterminately as "second," "third," and so on). Neither the absence of the appellative "good" on the second day—commonly considered as due to a copyist's error[6]—nor the minimal aberration between the lengths of the fourth and fifth days disturbs the overall pattern.

While classification of the creations ends with the sixth day, the text concludes with the Sabbath, which is described as the time when "the heaven and the earth were finished" and when "Elohim rested from all His work of creation." The seventh day is thus clearly set off from the *work* of the previous six. Its repose and calm stand in stark contrast to the acts of the days of creation: the Sabbath is a day of "rest" (as opposed to the predominance of "making" on the other days), a day blessed as a whole (as opposed to the blessings of the specific works of creation on the fifth and sixth days).

Most of all, the rest of the Sabbath day stands out against the dark silence of the primordial void. Between the stillness of the prologue and the calm of the epilogue there is a world of difference. The first silence precedes time, the second sanctifies it. The torpid waste of the primal beginning has been transformed through the creative acts of divine will and action. The completed work of creation becomes the new context for all that will follow. The Sabbath, at the end of the work of creation, also stands "at the beginning" of all new and future creations. The Sabbath, simultaneously a completion and a transition, marks the end of divine creation and the transfer of the earthly dominion to mankind. This dominion, as foretold in vv.28-30, is the context of the postcreation narratives which follow.

But whereas the orderly presentation of the creation of the world suggests an inherently logical sequence, commentators have long been perplexed. If God created light on the first day, what was created on the fourth? And if God prepared grass and seed on the third day, what was created on the sixth? Undoubtedly, one might contend that the light of the first day and the seeds of the third are merely potentialities with respect to the actualities of the luminaries and shoots of the fourth and sixth days, respectively.

A careful reading of Genesis 1:1-2:4*a* suggests, however, that the interrelationship between the separate acts of creation is both more complex and more simple than the surface sequence of days. Indeed, the medieval Jewish exegete Rashi already responded to the problems of determining the precise order of created elements in Genesis 1 when he maintained that one cannot understand this text strictly in terms of its literal continuity: "Scripture has not taught anything regarding the sequential order (lit., "the order of first and last")." But Rashi's remarks do not provide an explanation of the overall poetics of the passage. He was concerned primarily with the theological emphasis of Genesis 1 on the lordship of Elohim over all life, lands, and peoples.

A quite different approach to the text's literary underpinnings, which responds to its textual structure, can be found in a certain midrash which states that unlike the other creations, which were formed from either the upper or the lower spheres, man alone was created from them both. His creation on the sixth day thus balances the creation of heaven and earth (i.e., both spheres) on the first:

> How? On the first day He created heaven and earth, from the upper and lower [spheres]. On the second He created a firmament from the upper [spheres]. On the third He created grass and seeds from the lower [spheres]. On the fourth He created the lights from the upper [spheres]. On the fifth day He created from the lower [spheres]: "let the waters swarm." On the sixth day He created mankind [lit. "the man"]—his body from the earth and his spirit from heaven, so as to "tip the scales" among His creations.[7]

A modern version of this "argument from design," proposed by U. Cassuto, also focuses on the inner symmetry of the days of creation, but it has the merit of including the Sabbath day within its scheme. He suggested the following structure:[8]

day	1 light	2 (firmament separating) sea and heaven	3 dry land and seed
	4 luminaries	5 birds and fish; sea swarmers (creatures of heaven & sea)	6 land animals and mankind

7 Sabbath

This pattern shows the harmony and order of Genesis 1:1–2:4*a*. The first three days present the creation in its generalities, and the second three present those of its features which specifically impinge upon the human habitat. Man, created on the sixth day, is the steward of the lower order. Made in the "image and visage" of God, mankind has dominion over birds, fish, reptiles, and other animals. This symmetry of functions between God and man, together with the coordinated balance of the acts of creation, combine to disclose the text's inner logic and its teaching of a harmonious, orderly creation.

The emergent symmetry of the text (3 days plus 3 days plus 1 day) also suggests that the concluding Sabbath day is the culmination of this creation account. The acts of creation are the works of God; on the seventh day He ceased from work and rested. The entire creation account is thus theocentric: Elohim is the subject; He is the singular agent of will; He has created everything, including man. Accordingly, while man has a special position within the divine economy, and while man and women are formed in the "image and visage" of God Himself, Genesis 1:1-2:4a is not anthropocentric. Man is but a creature in the creation of the Creator, Elohim. The Sabbath is the conclusion, culmination, and witness to His work of creation (cf. Exodus 20:8-11).

The liturgical dimension of Genesis 1:1-2:4a reinforces this perception of the centrality of the Sabbath day. The refrain: "There was setting; there was dawning: day x," which concludes each of the first six days of the creation, anticipates the distinctiveness of the seventh day:

The heaven and the earth were finished and all therein.

Elohim finished	His work	on the seventh day;
And He rested from	His work	on the seventh day.
Elohim blessed		the seventh day;
And He set it apart.		
For on that day		
Elohim rested from all His work		of creation.

Clearly, this seventh paragraph of seven paragraphs, telling of the seventh day of the seven days of creation, is styled as a liturgical celebration of divine rest and the completed creation.[9] Its importance may well stem from a historical need to legitimate the Sabbath day and the seven-day week by locating them at the primordial time of the creation of the world. The ancient Israelite was bidden to work six days and, in acknowledgement of God's creation, to rest on the seventh and sanctify it (Exodus 20:8-11).

Although there is no other comprehensive account like

Genesis 1:1-2:4*a* in the Bible, a broad variety of creation imagery appears throughout Scripture. These are of two broad types: those which utilize the specific language of Genesis 1:1-2:4*a*, and those which reflect independent literary efforts and traditions. With respect to the first type, one instance is particularly striking. For a close reading of the closing chapters of the Book of Exodus discloses unmistakable echoes of the language of Genesis 1:1-2:4*a*. Indeed, as Martin Buber long ago noted, a series of key verbal parallels exists between the account of the creation of the world and the description of the building of the tabernacle in the desert (compare Genesis 1:31; 2:1; 2:2; 2:3 with Exodus 39:43; 39:32; 40:33; and 39:43, respectively). Thus "Moses saw all the work" which the people "did" in constructing the tabernacle; "and Moses completed the work" and "blessed" the people for all their labors. By this series of intertextual allusions, Buber suggested, a final compositor wished to direct the attentive hearer-reader ("Hörleser") to a correspondence between world-building and shrine-building, and therewith convey his theological insight that it is the task of mankind to extend and complete on earth the divine work of creation.[10]

These observations may be extended. First, the shift in emphasis from divine work in Genesis 2:1-3 to human work in Exodus 39-40 is indicated in two ways: by the fact that Moses is presented as subject of the actions performed; and by the fact that the rare expression *ruaḥ 'elohim* ("wind/spirit of Elohim") appears in Genesis 1:2, just prior to the transformation of the desolate waste into a world, as well as in Exodus 31:3, in connection with Bezalel's inspired role in the construction of the tabernacle. Second, it is most striking that both contexts place singular and decisive emphasis on Sabbath rest. In keeping with the aforenoted shift from divine to human action, the stress in Genesis 2:1-3 is on divine rest, whereas the emphasis in Exodus 31:12-17 and 35:2-3 is on human cessation from labor. And third, there is the arresting fact that the desert tabernacle was erected on the first day of the first month of the year (Exodus 40:2,17). Manifestly, then, the building of the tabernacle has been presented in the image of the creation of the world, and signified as an extension of a process begun at the creation.

This striking inner-biblical link between the creation the building of the tabernacle gains decided significance from a comparative point of view. For not only does the ancient

Mesopotamian creation epic *Enuma elish* feature the erection of shrines for the successive kingly rules of the two victorious creator-gods Ea and Marduk (I:71-77; VI:51-70), but a similar scenario, focused on the victor-god Ba'al, underlies the *Ba'al and Anat* cycle of Canaanite mythology as well (II AB i:10-11; v:62-vi:59). In fact, once isolated as a mythic pattern, the conjunction of elements referring to a primordial theomachy between the forces of creative order and watery chaos, and the subsequent erection of a shrine for the enthronement of the victorious god, is also found refracted in several biblical texts (cf. Psalms 29:3, 10; 74:12-17; 89:10-15; 93:1-4).[11]

However, these observations in no way diminish the singular reflex of this literary pattern in Genesis 1:1-Exodus 40:38. For in contrast with ancient Near Eastern versions, the temporal framework of Genesis 1:1-Exodus 40:38 includes not only primordial time but the long course from the universal history of mankind (Genesis 1-11) to the divine revelation and covenant with Israel at Sinai (Exodus 19-24). Accordingly, Genesis 1:1-Exodus 40:38 represents a remarkable transformation and historicization of an ancient mythic structure. The new beginning signified by the creation of the world is concluded by a symbolic renewal of that creation when the creator is built a dwelling on earth by His creatures. Divine lordship thus becomes an event on earth, and is not simply restricted to a primordial era or a cosmic realm. At the same time, this ancient mythic structure, and the verbal correspondences already noted between Genesis 2:1-3 and Exodus 39-40, serve severally to valorize the Israelite institution of a priestly tabernacle by placing it within an order of signification whose very origin is the beginning of the world.

As noted, another broad type of creation imagery, reflecting independent literary features, recurs in the diverse genres of biblical literature. Characteristic references occur in the prophets (e.g., Isaiah 27:1-2; 40:12-26; 45:18-19; 51:9-11; Habakkuk 3), in wisdom literature (e.g., Proverbs 8:22-32; Job 38-39), and in psalms (e.g., Psalms 8; 74:12-17; 89:6-13; 104; 136:4-9; 148). All attest to God's primordial power. In several, YHWH, the God of Israel, manifests His primordial might by routing antagonistic sea monsters *before* the creation itself.

> YHWH, God of the cosmic host, Who is like You?
> Mighty YaH, Your power is roundabout You.
> You subjected arrogant Yam (Sea)—

Breaking his waves as they reached up against You.
You hewed Rahab like a corpse—
Routing your enemies with Your mighty arm. (Psalms 89:9-12)

Similar passages can be found in Isaiah 27:1-2; 51:9-11; Habakkuk 3:8-11, 14-15; and Psalms 74:13-14. The monsters referred to, Yam and Rahab, also appear elsewhere in the Bible, along with other monsters—Nachash, Tanin and Leviathan—names which, like the battle descriptions themselves, bear a striking similarity to ones found in ancient Canaanite myths.[12] Elements also recall the story of the divine creator-hero Marduk in the Mesopotamian creation-epic, *Enumah elish*. Before the creation of the world, Marduk fought and defeated both the sea-monster Tiamat and her cohorts with winds (IV:42-48, 96-100) and a net (IV:41, 95, 112). These various features are also reflected in vestigial biblical creation traditions. Job 9:13, for example, explicitly refers to the "battle-cohorts of Rahab" subdued in a primordial blast of divine fury, and Job 26:12-13—set within an extensive creation passage—reflects a primal battle through a mixture of wind, wisdom and other imagery:

He quelled Yam (Sea) by His might,
    and squashed Rahab with His wisdom;
By His wind-blast He ensnared Yam,
    His arm lanced scaley Nachash (sea monster).

In this battle, as in biblical parallels, the dramatic imagery is used to enhance YHWH's power.

It must also be noted that the creation traditions scattered throughout biblical literature were utilized for diverse purposes. Thus many of the aforementioned texts (and also Psalms 104:25-26) cite the primordial battle of YHWH with a sea monster as prologue to a request for, or prophecy of, a remanifestation of divine power against evildoers and antagonists of the Israelites in history. These citations seek to "remind" God of His ancient power, or to invoke or prophesy it in the present for a renewed creation. Indeed, it is this very paradigm of once-wrought power that gives the psalmist confidence in his petition and the prophet assurance in his forecast. Just as the forces of anticosmos were once destroyed at the beginning, for the sake of a beginning, so is God addressed as the One through whom the harmony of creation can again be established. In other instances, biblical creation traditions serve other purposes—polemical (e.g., Isaiah 40:12-

26), theological (e.g., Isaiah 45:18-19), or didactic (e.g., Proverbs 8:22-32).

To sum up, the various non-Genesis creation traditions utilize poetic imagery and diverse sequences for the order of created things. They contain no references to a set order of "days" and do not mention the Sabbath day at all. By contrast Genesis 1:1-2:4*a*, highly stylized and nonpoetic in formulation, is deliberate about the order and numeration of the events of creation, and culminates on the Sabbath day. Second, the dramatic imagery of a precreation battle-victory by the protagonist creator over a monstrous antagonist clearly circulated in many forms in ancient Israel. It is starkly counterpointed by the nondramatic expression of divine power in Genesis 1:1-2:4*a*, where no antagonist is depicted. Indeed, the turbulence of this oft-recorded primordial battle fully contrasts with the orderly calm of the opening creation account in the Book of Genesis. This point may be succinctly set forth by recalling attention to the frequent references to the *tanin(im)-* sea dragon(s) in precreation battle traditions in the Bible (note Isaiah 27:1; 51:9; Psalms 74:13). The *taninim* are turbulent, restive and antagonistic creatures that must be quelled by the Creator's might. Their presentation fully contrasts with the reference in Genesis 1:21 to Elohim's creation of the great *taninim*, monsters whom God "blesses" and called "good."[13]

A final comparative implication between Genesis 1:1-2:4*a* and non-Genesis creation traditions may be noted. The utilization of combat imagery by the prophets and psalmists—as prologues to remanifestations of divine combative power in history—underscores the fact that Genesis 1:1-2:4*a* is presented as an ahistorical text from first to last. The Sabbath rest is a divine moment. It contains no historical vantage point which suggests that the created order has been ruptured by postcreation human antagonists and is therefore in need of repair. Genesis 1:1-2:4*a* is written as a prologue to history. In contrast to the disorder and disharmony of human creatures on earth, the opening biblical passage seeks to enforce the theological value of a primal order and harmony created by God. Its focus on an uncompromised divine will in a blessed creation counterpoints the ensuing texts which focus on human will and the despoliation of the earth (Genesis 2:4*b*-11:32). It is within this postcreation perspective of a created harmony ruptured and disordered by man in history that the aforenoted psalms and prophecies stand.

The transition from the opening biblical text in Genesis 1:1–2:4*a*, which deals with cosmic harmony, to the human turbulence which follows in the succeeding texts (Genesis 2:4*b*–11:32), is effected by a literary-editorial device. Genesis 2:4*a* ends, "This is the account of heaven and earth when they were created." And Genesis 2:4*b* begins, "On the day when YHWH-Elohim made earth and heaven..." The first text ends where the second begins: with the earth. The reader is thus made to cross over from the opening creation prologue (Genesis 1:1–2:4*a*) to the primeval cycle of mankind at its origins. The earth-centered creation tradition of Genesis 2:4*b*–25, which refers to the planting for man of a garden in Eden, now serves as a more immediate creation prologue to the acts of man in this primordial paradise.

2. Genesis 2:4*b*-11:32 /
The Primeval Cycle

I

Genesis 2:4*b*-25 has been recognized since antiquity as a distinct creation-tradition. Indeed, Philo, a Jewish philosopher and Bible scholar of ancient Alexandria (first century, C.E.), already noted differences of focus, detail and sequence between it and Genesis 1:1-2:4*a*.[1] All this is undoubtedly real; but one should not for that reason overlook the contextual fact that 2:4*b*-25 purports to provide, retrospectively, new details concerning the creation just described. The emphasis is on the fertile, nourished earth which precedes the creation of man and is "for" him. The narrative moves swiftly from the time of creation "before" man (vv.4*b*-6) to the time of his creation and placement in the earthly paradise of Eden (vv.7-15).

A geography of primordial space is thus mapped out which serves to supplement Genesis 1:1-2:4*a*. The natural harmony and bounty of the created earth are symbolized by a garden in the center of creation, where two semimagical trees embody and preserve the deepest mysteries of creation: the mysteries of life and knowledge. The perfection of this primordial space is further symbolized by four streams which enrich the four quadrants of the earth. The prototype of this symbolic image is often found in ancient religious iconography: a navel releasing life-giving water to the four corners of creation, together with a world mountain linking heaven and earth.[2] This image of a cosmic mountain is only indirectly suggested in Genesis 2:10-14, by its reference to the streams' downward flow. A later reflex of the Eden motif (Ezekiel 28:11-19) preserves this component more explicitly: The Garden is found on a "mountain of God" (v. 14).[3] It is undoubtedly on such a primal landscape, sustained by providential fertility, that man is placed in Genesis 2:15.

The next textual movement in the chapter dramatically disrupts this image of harmony and integration. In verses 16-17 YHWH-Elohim commands the man who tends the garden as follows: "You may eat, as you will, from every tree of the garden, except the tree of the knowledge of good and evil; for whensoever you eat from it you shall die." The reader is confronted with a confusion of details and meaning. In the first textual movement, v.9, two trees were mentioned; in v.17 only one is referred to. Is this an editorial discrepancy, or is it intentional—i.e., does it serve to "set up" the reader's expectations that this tree would be the one from which the man would eat? What is the relationship between the acquisition of knowledge and death? Could the man, who knew nothing about knowledge, or life, or restraint, have been expected to understand this divine prohibition? Surely the very commandment is confusing and unexpected.

However, when Genesis 2:4ff. is read together with Genesis 1:1–2:4a, the turn of events effected by the prohibition becomes more understandable. The very hierarchy of the divine dominion described in the opening lines of Genesis, particularly with respect to Elohim's lordship over man, implies a world of boundaries and subservience. And more: the blessing to man in Genesis 1:28ff. regarding his dominion over the earthly realm implies that man is a creature with a will. The latent tension between human and divine will is made manifest with the prohibition in vv.16–17. When God informs man of the fixed hierarchies between creator and creature, and so sets limits to human will, He provokes a cognitive paradox. It is precisely the imposition of this prohibition that stimulates man as a willful, autonomous agent.

The text of Genesis 2:4bff. thus lends itself to the following reading: "Man" here is "everyman," insofar as he is born and finds himself in a sustaining environment. His postnatal world is one of sustenance and harmony. It is only with the first authoritative prohibition that limits to his experience are introduced. God's command is addressed to man's "orality," that is to his childhood desire to "incorporate" knowledge and life through his mouth. The divine command impinges on his freedom to "take things in," to "absorb" experience. It also stimulates the will by creating a distance between man's self and the objects of the world, a distance to be bridged by a new act of will which reappropriates the world by distinguishing and naming its objects. Thus the narrative sequence of naming the creatures, which immediately follows the prohibition in vv.18ff, fits psychologically into this textual scenario of human dominance of the earth. The human creature not only differentiates itself from its environment through the symbolic medium of language, but establishes therewith diverse orders of differentiation as well. In so doing, man-the-steward, like God-the-creator, creates a world with words.

A profound intuition would thus seem to underlie this text, one which sees a symmetry between a world established and hierarchically differentiated by divine language, and into which the Man is placed, and the corresponding task of this Man and mankind to further differentiate this divine syntax and establish new orders and meanings. The result is an ever more penetrating paradox: The human creature is at once profoundly alienated from the world by the inherent arbitrariness and metaphorical quality of all linguistic designations; and yet such a one is, nonetheless, the vital and necessary shaper of syntaxes of meaning on earth.

Nevertheless, the differentiation of self from the world of things, and the differentiations made within this very world of things remain, at this textual stage, only an incipient possibility. The primordial womb of Eden still envelops the human creature forming within it. And so Genesis 2:4*b*–25 concludes (v.25) with the pregnant notice that both men and women were yet *'arumim*, "naked" and unashamed. The innocence of this image points towards the next chapter, Genesis 3, where the tempting serpent is called *'arum*, "wily" (v.1), and where man and woman know that they are *'erumim*, "naked" (v.5), after transgressing the interdiction of Genesis 2:15–16. Once again, as was the case with Genesis 2:4*a* and 2:4*b*, key words serve to link the narratives.

II

Genesis 3 deals with the serpent's temptation of the woman, Eve, in the Garden of Eden. She succumbs to her desire for the forbidden fruit from the tree of the knowledge of good and evil, apparently believing the serpent's words that on eating it she would become divine. She then gives the fruit to her husband, who also eats of it. Immediately thereafter both the man and the woman become ashamed of their nakedness, clothe themselves, and hide from God. God confronts His creatures with their transgression, curses them and, in order to prevent their eating from the tree of life as well, banishes them from the garden. A fiery sword is placed at its entry to prohibit all access.

Although the scenario of this chapter seems relatively straightforward on the surface, a number of questions arise. What is being described in this text? Who are the characters depicted? Is the text a literal, or moral, or theological teaching on the relationship between sin and punishment or the question of free human will and responsibility? Or does it touch on other issues too?

To answer these questions it is necessary first to develop some understanding of the content and structure of Genesis 3, which, despite its clear progression from chapter 2, stands mysteriously closed within its own sphere of meaning. The text opens with the unexpected appearance of the serpent, who contradicts the divine command (v.4) and further interprets its motivation. He tells the woman (whose knowledge of the prohibition is not explained) that God has forbidden the fruit of the tree of the knowledge of good and evil,

> Because Elohim (God) knows that as soon as you eat of it your eyes will be opened, and you will *be like Elohim* (God/gods?) *knowing good and evil* (v.5)

The key elements here, "Elohim knows/knowing" and "be like Elohim," recur at the conclusion of the story of the forbidden fruit, where the fear stated by the serpent, that mankind "will be like Elohim," becomes a reality:

> And YHWH Elohim said: Surely, the man has become *like one of us knowing good and evil*....(v.22)

In addition to the progressive development from the beginning of the narrative to its conclusion, there is also marked contrast. In its opening section the main speaker is the serpent; in the closing statement it is YHWH-Elohim who speaks. In the beginning there is the lie, the challenge, the provocation of jealousy and resentment; in the end God has the final, fateful verdict on man's action, banishing him from the garden. Genesis 3 moves from temptation to rebellion and its consequences.

Within this structure, a psychological drama unfolds. The serpent seduces the woman to eat of the tree by raising her suspicion that God's prohibition is arbitrary and that human will is being inhibited merely to guarantee divine superiority. God does not want man to be "like" him, says the serpent—a provocation that undoubtedly stimulates Eve's resentment. Her resistance to the appeal of the fruit is immediately lowered. She eats from the tree and seduces her husband into disobedience as well. Repressed desire has been stimulated and sated, and the eyes of mankind are "opened" as the serpent had predicted.

With the eating of the fruit, limits have been transgressed. Open eyes, knowledge, and shame replace the original innocence of life in Eden. The couple sees itself in a new way; in their new self-consciousness they impose restraints on themselves. Ashamed of their nudity, they quickly clothe themselves. This new self-awareness further manifests itself as fear in the face of the prohibiting authority, God, and guilt for one's transgressions. The man hides from both his accuser and himself. When Elohim confronts him, he attempts to dissociate himself from the consequences of his behavior and so lies to himself. The man further projects his own guilt outward and blames the woman, who in turn blames the serpent. This guilt-and-blame sequence (vv.9–13) which inverts the original narrative order of serpent-woman-man (vv.1–6), recurs in the succession of curses (vv.14–19). The serpent who was "more sly than all the beasts of the field" (v.1) becomes "more cursed than all the beasts of the field" (v.14); and desire and contention would ever remain between him and the woman (v.15). The woman, for her part, is further cursed with the pain of pregnancy and childbirth *('itzvonekh; 'etzev.)*. And the man, who would dominate her, is himself punished with a cursed earth to till in pain *('itzavon)*—until death. The fruit of the knowledge of good and evil is pain, enmity, shame, and death.

Genesis 3 thus deals with the profound interconnection between knowledge and death. The promised punishment of death for transgression in 2:15–16 is not only mortality but also the human awareness of mortality. The perception of opposites and distinctions, the knowledge of good and evil, no matter how life-building and "eye-opening," also includes the consciousness of death. With the banishment from Eden, man is, through consciousness and self-awareness, alienated from primal simplicity; he is set forever among choices and opposites.[4] The boundaries of knowledge have been transgressed and their burdens made manifest. To know pain, to be conscious of desire, and to anticipate death are, from the perspectives of this text, indicative of mankind's rupture from an aboriginal, primal harmony. The curses cannot be redressed; a flaming sword henceforth bars the way to Eden. Man has become the being we ourselves are: a mortal creature set within the conflicting turmoil of desire and choice.

This narrative of human origins suggests that the dramatic actions of the first man mask the ever-recurrent reality of "everyman"—insofar as he is a choosing being. "Everyman" experiences versions of the acts of the man, woman and serpent. Woman represents that side of humankind which reaches out toward the world and its seductions; she symbolizes that part which desires to incorporate the variety of "life" without inhibition or interdiction. The serpent symbolizes the instinctual, rebellious urges fueling that desire and "cleverly" concocting justifications for it.[5]

With the eating of the fruit, the inner conflicts of desire emerge, and internalized restraints are broken. The irony is that it is just man's innate quality as a creature of will that contains the very seeds of his own destruction. He reaches for life and knowledge and is destroyed by their insatiable urge. This internal drama is expressed through the external dramatic scenario of Genesis 3.

This narrative of man's origins plunges us into another even deeper mystery: the origin of evil. The rupture of the primal and beneficent god-given harmony "at the beginning" represents, from a theological point of view, the emergence of evil into existence. But who was responsible? A close reading of Genesis 3 provides two answers. Evil enters the world through man and his choices as a creature of free will. Man can serve God and the creation, or he can disobey. The dialogues of Genesis 2:16–17 and 3:1ff. dramatize these possibilities. Man can and does choose against God's orderly creation. Such a perspective constitutes an anthropology of evil, insofar as man introduces disharmony into the order of God's creation through active rebellion or passive complicity. Man finds himself as a creature in a world with commandments and limits, lies and seductions. His energies and desires can be perverted; he can choose against God, himself and his world through self-destructive overreaching. Man reaps the curses of his own misdirected will.

But while the dominant focus in Genesis 2:4*b*–25 is on the first man's rebellion, something remains to be explained. Can it not equally be said that the man is seduced into rebellion by a clever creature who is part of God's creation, the serpent? Or does the serpent perhaps represent some fragment of the inchoate waste and void, some vestige of a primordial drive within nature which remained independent even after God's creation?

From this second perspective the origin of evil is considered not simply a result of misdirected will but as lying deep within the "nature" of things despite the created "order." The serpent represents that part of the world and man resistant to a fixed order. It appears to be outside of man, stimulating his desires. But it is also a primordial, serpentine chaos coiled in the well of being. The serpent is *with* us in the world, *without* us in the world, and *within* us in the world. Insofar as this force exists within God's creation, the text hints—however mutely—at a theology of evil at the same time as it emphasizes man's responsibility for the existence of evil.[6]

By this double exposure, the narrative of Genesis 3 crystallizes a paradox: on the one hand man receives a gracious earth which, by his willfulness, he perverts; on the other hand, that perversion or evil seems inherent in the created world itself, as symbolized by the serpent. This paradox is brought to consciousness by the narrative but is not resolved. These issues of evil, will and choice are reconsidered from a broader interpersonal perspective in Genesis 4.

III

Then the man knew his wife, Eve; and
she conceived and bore Cain, saying:
"I have begotten a person with YHWH."
And she continued to bear: his brother, Abel.

Abel was a shepherd; Cain worked the earth.
After some time it happened that Cain brought YHWH an
   offering
From the fruits of the earth,
Whereas Abel brought, for his part, from
the first-born of his sheep and their fat;
But YHWH had regard for Abel and his offering.
He disregarded Cain and his offering;
This greatly infuriated Cain and he became downcast.
YHWH said to Cain: "Why are you furious and downcast?
If you act well, you can bear it,* but if you don't, sin crouches
at the ready; its urge will be towards you, but you can dominate
   it."

Cain then spoke to his brother Abel
and, when they were in the field, he up and killed his brother
   Abel.
YHWH said to Cain: "Where is your brother Abel?"

---

*Literally, "there is bearing of/raising of"; for *se'et* is a construct infinitive without (pro)nominal object. But even if the implied object is "face," yielding a common West-Semitic idiom for "uplift," the concern is still with the emotion aroused. See below, and note 8.

And he said: "I don't know; am I my brother's guardian?"
Then He said: "What have you done? Behold, your brother's blood
Cries out to me from the earth.
Therefore: Be you cursed by the earth which opened its mouth
to receive your brother's blood from your hand.
When you work the earth it will no longer give its yield to you.
A vilified vagabond will you be over the land."
Cain said to YHWH: "My misdeed is too much to bear.
If you banish me over the earth, to be hidden from your presence,
then I shall be a vilified vagabond over the land
and whoever will catch me will wreak deadly revenge!"
YHWH said to him: "If so, whoever kills Cain will be revenged
   sevenfold."
Then YHWH gave Cain a sign so that whoever might catch Cain
would not kill him.
Then Cain left YHWH's presence and settled in Nod,
eastward of Eden.

While Genesis 3 is an inner-psychic drama, these verses from
chapter 4 (vv.1–16) are a sociological extension of the same
concerns. The two texts are independent, yet interrelated by
theme and language.

Genesis 4 opens with a brief genealogy noting the birth of
Cain and Abel. In itself, this witness to the progeneration of
life links back to the curses of the preceding chapter (3:16):
that humans would be mortal and give birth in pain *('etzev)*.
The language of this birth notice—"then the man knew *[yada']*
his wife, Eve, and she conceived and bore Cain [who]...
worked the earth [lit., "was a worker of the earth," *'oved
'adamah]*"—is subtly phrased to allude both to the couple's
eating from the tree of knowledge *(da'at)*, with their subsequent knowledge *(vayyede'u)* of their nakedness, and to the
curse of Adam, who was banished from the garden "to work
the earth *[la'avod et ha-'adamah]*."

At the close of the narrative in Genesis 4, Cain tells God that
if He would "banish" him (stem: *garash*, v.14) because of the
murder of his brother, Abel, Cain would "be hidden" (v.14)
from His presence. This is reminiscent of Genesis 3, in which
Adam and Eve "hid" from God and were later "banished"
(stem: *garash*; v.24) from His paradise. In the end, Cain was
banished "eastward of Eden" (v.16), even as Adam finally
settled "east of the Garden of Eden" (v.24). This repetition of
phrases and features links Genesis 3 and 4 and provides access
to the latter's meaning.

While the same psychodynamics of will and choice occur in

both Genesis 3 and 4:1-16, there is a difference. In Genesis 3 the dynamic occurs on an interior, psychical plane, but in 4:1-16 it is transposed to an exterior, familial one. The same tension of choice and temptation recurs, but in the Cain-Abel episode it is not only a private event but one with interpersonal-social consequences as well.

Genesis 4:3-16 involves the murder of a brother. However, reference to this murder is minimal; a terse note in v.8, between a long prologue (vv.3-7) and a long epilogue (vv.9-16), both of which include extensive dialogues between God and Cain. Similarly, v.8, midway between them, opens with reference to a dialogue between Cain and his brother. The speech, however, is not preserved in the received Hebrew Bible; and in many traditional manuscripts only a blank space is left between "and Cain spoke to his brother Abel" and the reference to the murder itself. While many generations of readers have supplemented Cain's words with their own meaning projections, no direct help is forthcoming from the text. Nevertheless, the language of this broken verse does serve to emphasize the fraternal dimension of this murder: the word *'ah*, "brother," which had previously been mentioned only in the birth announcement of v.2, is twice repeated in v.8 and recurs with great insistency to the end of the text. There can be no doubt that the murder of a brother is the linchpin of the entire narrative. But what motivated it?

The text opens in darkness. Why has God accepted the gift of Abel and not that of Cain? Because Cain was a farmer like his father and was reaping his father's curse (3:23)? Was Cain's intention less pure, or did he offer an inferior sacrifice? Generations of interpreters have labored over the question. But is it not just in this darkness that the clue lies? The temptation is already there, from the beginning, mysteriously. The tension of Cain's dilemma and temptation is that the conflict arises inexplicably, with no apparent sense to the choice of God. Cain's battle is to gain internal control over external non-sense. He must allay his frustrations at manifest injustice so as to overcome the trial with dignity. With a keen penetration into the exasperation of Cain, but with little sympathy for Cain's lack of faith before the absurd, an ancient rabbinic legend attributes these words to him: "There is neither justice nor Judge [in this world]!"[7]

In Genesis 4:3-16, God appears as a counterforce to Cain's inner turbulence, telling him to withstand the anger he feels towards Abel. "If you act well, you can bear it [i.e., the temptation], but if you don't, sin crouches at the ready."[8] This image of sin recalls Genesis 3; coiled now at the root of Cain's will, the serpent is in external enmity with man, as was foretold (3:15). Cain may "subdue" it, but only for a while, because the enmity is eternal, and a constant alertness and overcoming are necessary. But Cain succumbs. He is cursed and banished from his post-Eden environment, the social context of his family.

The Cain–Abel narrative picks up the inner dynamic of Genesis 3 through repetition of key words and images. Students of the Bible ranging over time from the ancient rabbis to the modern scholar U. Cassuto have contributed to the following list of correspondences.[9] My schematization of Genesis 4:3–16 follows the narrative sequence. The parallels in Genesis 3 are aligned to it.

	Genesis 4:3–16	*Genesis 3*
1.	"Then the man knew [*yada'*] his wife, Eve"	"and they knew [*va-yede'u*] that they were naked"
2.	temptation dramatized through coiled, serpentine sin	temptation dramatized through the serpent
3.	"its [the serpentine-sin's] urge [*teshuqato*] will be towards you"	"your [the woman's] desire-urge [*teshuqatek*] will be towards your husband"
4.	"but you can dominate [*timshol*] it;"	"but he will dominate [*yimshol*] you;"
5.	"where is ['*ay*] your brother?"	"where are you ['*ayeka*]?"
6.	"be you cursed by the earth ['*arur 'atta min ha-'adamah*]"	"cursed be the earth ['*arura ha-'adamah*] because of you;"
7.	"when you work the earth [*ta-'avod et ha-'adameh*] it will no longer give its yield to you"	"briars and thistles will sprout for you to work the earth [*la-'avod et ha-'adameh*]"
8.	"you have banished [*gerashta*] me"	"He banished [*va-yegaresh*] the man"

9. "I will be hidden [*'essater*] from your presence [*paneka*]"

"then the man and his wife hid [*va-yithabbe*] from the presence [*p'nei*] of YHWH Elohim"

10. "eastward of Eden [*qidmat 'eden*]"

"east(ward) of the garden of Eden [*miqqedem le-gan 'eden*]"

The parallelism of the texts is thoroughgoing: there is temptation, desire, conflict, crime, punishment, and exile east of Eden. Like Genesis 3, Genesis 4:3–16 serves notice that man acts evilly in a world that—inexplicably—enables him to do so. The presentation of the serpentine temptation as an interior force in the latter text recalls the earlier suggestion that the serpent is both part of man's (inner) nature, and part of the nature of things (which, of course, includes man).

In effect, Genesis 4:3–16 exemplifies the eternal enmity of the serpent according to the curse of 3:16. Whereas the temptation in Genesis 3 affected selfish, private desires, that in Genesis 4 is of a more social type, born of frustration and anger. The motivational power of desire and curiosity in Genesis 3 thus takes on the interpersonal forms of aggression, rage, and revenge in 4:3–16.

Its sequel (vv.17–26) adds an ironic, shrewd insight. Cain is credited with founding the first city, and his descendants become the producers of music and metalwork. The juxtaposition of these cultural developments to Cain's genealogy suggests that the editor was both aware of the energies which build civilization, and cynical about the power and pride which drive man to civilize his life and create tools and culture, and that can recoil on themselves and explode in death-dealing anger. The energy of Cain the farmer can, if blocked, erupt in self-righteous resentment and indignation. Desire and restraint are shown to be locked in mortal, self-destructive combat. Civilization is built and destroyed by discontent.

IV

The transition from the Cain–Abel episode to the genealogy of Cain is marked by the following verse (v.17): "then Cain knew his wife, and she conceived and bore Enoch...." This notice is identical with that marking the transition from the garden of Eden: "then the man knew his wife, Eve, and she conceived and bore Cain...." Indeed, the emphasis on genealogies, or *toledot*, together with a series of intersecting, independent narrative episodes, constitute the structure of the primeval cycle (Genesis 2:4*b*–11:32).

In the texts of Genesis 1:1–11:32, a series of narrative episodes set in primeval time interweave with a series of genealogical lists or *toledot* notices. Each of the narrative units from the creation, Eden, the temptation and banishment, the murder of Abel and Cain's exile, the Flood and cosmic regeneration, to the Tower of Babel and the dispersion of peoples—are self-contained entities which can be read separately. Their present integration in the Bible is the result of a creative coordination of traditions. It is noteworthy that several of the episodes have reflexes in ancient Mesopotamia texts but are not themselves part of a comprehensive epic cycle.

This literary independence of the various narratives stands in contrast to the *toledot* genealogies, which provide a coherent, consecutive chain from Adam to Abram. They link narratives and determine the basic movement of the entire cycle: the narrative episodes of Adam and his sons (Eden and post-Eden) are followed by genealogies down to Noah and the Flood; the narrative episodes of Noah and his sons (the Flood and its aftermath) are followed by genealogies down to the generation of the Tower of Babel; and that narrative is, in turn, followed by genealogies down to the time of Abram and his descendants.

These genealogies are not indiscriminately presented, but reflect instead a highly selective pruning of the genealogical tree from Adam, the first man, to Abram, son of Terah and descendant of Eber, and first patriarch of the covenant people of Israel. The primeval cycle must therefore be fully appreciated as a prologue to the episodes and genealogies of the patriarchs—Abram, Isaac, and Jacob. The movement is intentional and deliberate: from Adam to Abram, from the father of mankind to the father of one historical people.

To more fully appreciate the integration of the narratives and genealogies, one may view them in three exposures reflecting three different emphases. The first of these features, the genealogies, have their own deliberate momentum and pace: name after name, life after life, father and son, son and father. Their mark is continuity and generation. Their formal features are notices of birth, age, descendants, and death. As the genealogies cascade into history, there is both an increase in world population and a restricted focus to that line which produced Abram, the first father of the ancient Hebrews.

But side by side with the rapid litany of faceless, contentless names of the genealogies, the narrative episodes are fleshed out by the lives of several individuals in all their turbulence. In the narratives the names of the genealogy become willing and acting creatures: brother kills brother, group hates group, fathers bless and curse sons. Life, will, and desire pulse within these texts. And God is also present: in speech, response, blessing, and curse. Man is not alone but breathes in the presence of God.

The third exposure brings both episodes and genealogies into prominence, so that a reader perceives the counterpoint between faceless names and "face-full" episodes.

What is especially striking is the deep inner structure of theme and motif which integrates the various narratives, as can be seen in the following diagram:

I. Genesis 1:1-2:3—narrative of Creation, Order, Dominion and Rest.

Toledot —genealogies of Heaven and Earth (Genesis 2:4*a*)

II. Genesis 2:4*b*-3:24—narratives of Creation, Adam and Eve, Temptation, Willful Desire, Curse and Exile.

Toledot —genealogies (Genesis 4:1-2)

III. Genesis 4:3-16—narrative of Cain and Abel, Temptation, Willful Aggression, Divine Curse, and Exile.

Toledot —genealogies (Genesis 4:17-5:32)

IV. Genesis 6-9—narrative of Women and Gods, Temptation, and Desire, Aggression, Divine Destruction (Flood) and Re-creation (with subsequent blessings, infractions, and curses).

Toledot —genealogies (Genesis 10)

V. Genesis 11:1-9—narrative of Men and God (Tower of Babel), Temptation, Willful Desire, Aggression, Divine Punishment-Curse, Exilic-Dispersion.

Toledot —genealogies (Genesis 11:10-32)

V

The biblical account of Noah and the Flood has been traditionally assumed to begin with his genealogy in Genesis 6:9-10 ("These are the *toledot* of Noah...") and the subsequent divine anger at human injustice (vv.11-13), although many modern scholars have preferred to regard the episode as commencing earlier, in 6:5-7, in a parallel prologue which refers to human "evil" and the consequent divine decision to destroy mankind. Noah, who finds favor with the Lord (6:8) and is righteous in an evil time (6:9), is singled out to survive the dissolution by flood of all creation. He builds an ark according to divine specifications and, together with his immediate family, stocks it with exemplars of all animal life (6:14-7:9). As a cosmos in miniature, the ark providentially survives the universal destruction, so that its inhabitants can serve as the nucleus for a renewed world. The narrative closes with God's promise never again to destroy the earth because of mankind, and to restore the cycle of nature (8:21-22). The rainbow in the heavens is His eternal testimonial to this promise (9:11-17).

A complex weave of literary strands and common ancient Near Eastern imagery underlie the Flood account, which is integrated into the primeval cycle by the aforenoted genealogy of 6:9-10:

> These are the *toledot* of Noah
> (Noah was a just man, perfect in his generation;
> Noah walked constantly with Elohim):
> *Noah sired* three sons: *Shem, Ham, and Japhet.*

This genealogical notice recapitulates the earlier statement of Noah's progeny in 5:32,

> Now Noah was five hundred years old;
> and *Noah sired Shem, Ham, and Japheth.*

which follows a long list of world ancestors and heroes beginning with Seth, son of Adam (Genesis 5:6ff.). The literary pattern which emerges—of creation, development and degeneration of mankind, pre-Flood ancestors, and a flood—is one also known from the Mesopotamian *Atra-hasis Epic.*[10] It suggests that an ancient literary schema, which contained an antediluvian hero who survived a universal flood, has also affected the sequence of Genesis 1-9.

A more concentrated focus on the first genealogical notice of Noah in Genesis 5:32 reveals that he was born ten generations after Adam and ten generations before Abram. Noah and the Flood account thus stand at a climactic pivot in Genesis 1-11. Noah's link with Adam is further obvious from the popular name etymology which appears together with his birth announcement in 5:29:

> Lamech sired a son and called his name Noah, saying: "This one will comfort us from our work and painful toil on the earth which YHWH has cursed..."

The name "Noah" is thus not explained from the Hebrew verbal stem *nwh*, meaning "rest," as would be etymologically appropriate, but rather from the stem *nhm*, meaning "comfort." He was to give comfort "from our...painful toil [*'itzvon*] on the earth [*'adamah*] which YHWH has cursed [*'arerah*]." There can be no doubt that this text was intended to balance the curse to the first man, Adam in Genesis 3:17, where God stated: "The earth [*'adamah*] will be cursed [*'arurah*] on your account; you will eat from it through painful toil [*'itzavon*]."

Noah is thus portrayed as a new Adam, a provider of hope and comfort east of Eden. The full restorative possibilities adumbrated here remain unconsummated, however, for

> YHWH saw the great evil of mankind in the world, whose every impulse and thought is ever evil. Then YHWH regretted [*vay yinnahem*] having made mankind in the world, and He was troubled [*vayyit'atzev*] at heart. So YHWH said: "I shall wipe out mankind which I have made from off the earth, even man and beast, (earth) swarmer and bird of the sky; for I regret [*nihamtiy*] having made them." But Noah found favor with YHWH.

Through clever use of theme words, the language of the preceding text (6:5-8) recalls the etymology for Noah (5:29). But whereas the verbal stems *nhm* and *'tzv* were used in 5:29 to mean "comfort" and "painful toil," respectively, they are used in 6:5-8 to denote "regret" and "troubled." Noah, whose name forecast the restoration of the estate of mankind, is now (6:8) but meager comfort to a God furious with His creation.

As noted earlier, Genesis 6:5-8 is also considered to be a prologue to the Flood, and thus parallel to that in 6:9-13. Accordingly, the unexplained "evil" which mankind did (6:5) is clarified by the reference to *hamas*, "social violence," in v.13. This latter is offered as the motivation for the destruction of mankind, an act of divine retribution for acts of human injustice. The primordial fear of the whimsical eruption of

divine wrath and the consequent disruption of the natural
order—features well known from world folklore—are brought
here under rationalizing control. By directly linking divine
punishment to human evil, the narrator undercuts the terror
known to ancient Mesopotamians of whimsical, even narcissis-
tic gods. The aforementioned *Atra-hasis Epic*, in fact, speaks
of how the gods decided to destroy mankind when men's
increasing noise came to disturb their rest. Several drastic
measures follow, culminating in a universal flood.

Nevertheless, there does appear to be a second nonmoral
explanation of divine wrath in the biblical Flood account. The
repetition of the Noahide progeny in Genesis 5:32 and 6:9-10
isolates 6:1-8 as an independent antediluvian unit. This is a
significant observation, for it allows us to perceive that 6:5-8 is
not a fragmentary prologue to the Flood (parallel to vv.9-13)
but actually presents the consequence of the acts committed in
6:1-4, a mythological vestige portraying the mating between
divine beings and women of the earth.

> And it was when men began to increase over the earth that they
> sired daughters. And the gods saw that the daughters of man
> were beautiful, and took whomsoever they wished to wife.
>
> Then YHWH said: "My spirit will not protect mankind forever,
> for he is but flesh. Let him live 120 years."
>
> The divine giants lived then, and also after the gods coupled with
> the daughters of man. And they sired of them—heroes, ancestral
> men of renown-name.

This text states that after the event of mating YHWH limited
the life span of mankind. But is it not strange that He punished
humans for divine actions? And further: what was the nature
of the crime such that it elicited the punishment of reduced life
expectancy?

Given the thematic-structural fact that in both Genesis 3 and
Genesis 11:1-9 (the Tower of Babel) the concern is the testing
of divine-human limits, it would seem that in Genesis 6:1-4 the
crime is also one of testing and transgressing limits due to the
intercourse between human and divine beings. The danger
that mankind could become semidivine is made explicit in the
reference to the heroic progeny born of such a union.[11] This
event must be understood to have preceded the punishment in
v.3, wherein man's mortality is stressed and his life span
restricted to 120 years. The anger which these actions of
divine-human mating elicited led to God's further decision to

destroy mankind (vv.5-8). The fact that mankind and not the culprit divine-beings is punished in v.3 and vv.5-7 underscores the real danger: that humankind might circumvent the curse of Eden and "live forever" (Genesis 3:22).

Genesis 6:1-4 emerges from the dreamworld of collective memory. Recurrent fantasies of achieving divine longevity and heroic prowess are acted out on a primal landscape. As noted, the opening Genesis narratives depict recurrent testing of limits by mankind in its infancy. The human beings in these texts become the persons we are ourselves, mortal and caught in the web of life-determining choices. The divine responses to the acts of human "testing" still bear the traces of an authority which overresponds because of fear of competition from their dependents. Nevertheless, in the archaic language of these texts, a deep accommodation is achieved by God towards His creation. After the Flood God says, in words alluding both to pre-Flood considerations ("YHWH saw the...evil of mankind ...whose every impulse...is ever evil," 6:5-6) and the original curse to Adam ("the earth will be cursed on your account," 3:17):

> I shall no longer curse the earth on account of mankind, for the impulses of the mind of mankind are evil from childhood.

Following man's infractions and misdemeanors, God's wrath breaks forth and the cosmos is destroyed. The Flood is described as a reversal of the creation itself: "both the springs of the mighty deep [*tehom,* cf. Genesis 1:2] and the sluices of heaven were opened" (7:11). This anticreation imagery of the destruction is confirmed by the language used of the restoration, which is presented as a *new creation.* The description of the re-creation begins in Genesis 8:1-3, which describes how the wind of Elohim blew over the earth and stopped up the waters of the deep (cf. Genesis 1:2):

> And Elohim remembered Noah, and all the creatures and animals which were with him in the ark. And *Elohim brought a wind over the earth,* so that the waters abated. Thus the springs of the *deep [tehom]* and the sluices of the heavens were stopped up; and rain was withheld in the heavens. The waters began to recede from the earth, until they were diminished after 150 days.

This depiction recalls the biblical and ancient Near Eastern imagery of the primordial combat with the sea monster, noted in chapter 1 (cf. Psalms 74:12-15; 89:10-12; 104:6-10; 148:6). The imagery used here portrays Elohim's vigorous control

over the forces of the world, which can be ordered or unleashed
at His will. It is thus fitting that the sign of the covenant in
Genesis 9, after the reordering of the watery chaos, is the
bow—an ancient weapon of divine combat. The Bible often
presents God's intervention in history to defeat Israel's enemies
with the imagery of bows, arrows, and nets (note especially
Habakkuk 3:9ff.). Similar weapons were also employed by
Marduk in his cosmogonic battle against Tiamat.[12] The combat
bow in Genesis 9, however, is hung in the heavens—a sign of
divine promise and resignation. The world will no longer be
destroyed because of man's evil actions. Primordial fears are
put to rest.

The "recreation" motif begun in 8:1-3 concludes with the
renewal of mankind on a mountain (8:4) and recapitulates in
9:1-2, 6-7 the language of Genesis 1:26ff.:

> And Elohim blessed Noah and his sons, and said to them: "Be
> fruitful and multiply and fill the earth; and may your lordship
> and power rule the creatures of the earth, the birds of the
> heavens; and all that swarms on the earth and swims in the sea I
> have given to you...for man was created in the image of God. But
> be fruitful and multiply, swarm on the earth, and increase
> thereon."

Noah is thus portrayed as a new Adam in a renewed creation.
The hopes of comfort and consolation anticipated in 5:29 are
now consummated.

VI

After a brief description of events involving Noah's sons
(9:18ff.), the cycle continues with a genealogical "table of
nations" in Genesis 10. This genealogy links the Flood account
to the Tower of Babel episode in 11:1-9.

> And all the earth spoke one language and similar words. And it
> was when they traveled from the East that they came upon a
> valley in Shinar, and settled there. Then one person said to the
> other: "Come, let us form molds and light the kiln." So the mold
> hardened and the clay thickened. And they said: "Come, let us
> build a city and tower, with its top in the heavens, and so make
> ourselves a name, lest we be scattered over the earth."

> At that time YHWH descended to see the city and tower which
> the sons of man had built. YHWH said: "Indeed, all these are one
> people, one language for all. And just see what they've done.
> However, nothing of their plan will succeed. Come, let us descend

and garble their language, so that one cannot understand the language of the other."

Then YHWH scattered them over the earth, and they ceased building the city. Therefore it was called Babel, for YHWH had there babbled the language of all the earth, and scattered them thence over the earth.

The literary pericope, or unit, is thematically integrated with the preceding narrative episodes of the primeval cycle. It is linked to the surrounding genealogies by a framing device similar to that noted with respect to Genesis 5:32 and 6:9-10 (the genealogies of Noah). In the present case, the genealogy preceding the "Tower" episode in 10:31-32,

These are the sons of Shem according to their clans and languages, in their lands and groupings...after the Flood

is linked to that which follows it in 11:10:

These are the *toledot* of Shem...two years after the Flood.

The repetition serves a triple function: it continues the genealogies of Shem down to Abram; it continues the interlocking structure of *toledot* and narratives; and it isolates and frames the Tower of Babel episode as an independent unit. Interestingly, an ancient Mesopotamian parallel to the "Tower" episode also projects the origin of the division of languages into primordial time.[13] Characteristically, the Mesopotamian piece centers around the whim and ego of the gods, whereas the biblical episode shifts the focus to the aggression of man. As with the other narrative units of Genesis 1-11, man lives with the consequences of his own actions. He is not a helpless victim of divine whim.

In his analysis of this text, Martin Buber focused attention on such key words and phrases as "all the earth," let us "build," "city and tower," and the verb "to scatter," and on their recurrences.[14] The text opens with a reference to "all the earth," which is repeated at the end when the people are "scattered...over the face of the earth." The verb "to scatter" is used earlier in "lest we be scattered over the earth"; thus the people's earlier fear of being scattered is realized. The same balance of phrases occurs elsewhere. At the outset each says to the other: "let us build a city and tower." And, at the end, when God espies the "city and tower," He says to His pantheon: "Let us (go down)." Finally, the phrase "all the earth spoke one language," at the beginning of the selection, is alluded to at the end, in the punishment, when God "babbled" the language of mankind "and scattered them...over the earth."

The Tower of Babel episode can thus be diagrammed as a symmetrical composition. This was first noticed by Y. Raddai and, with various revisions, can be presented as follows:[15]

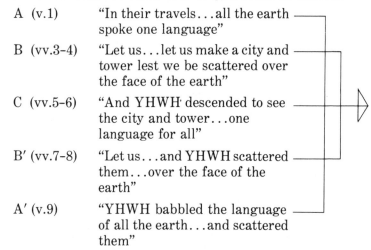

A (v.1)   "In their travels...all the earth spoke one language"

B (vv.3-4)   "Let us...let us make a city and tower lest we be scattered over the face of the earth"

C (vv.5-6)   "And YHWH descended to see the city and tower...one language for all"

B' (vv.7-8)   "Let us...and YHWH scattered them...over the face of the earth"

A' (v.9)   "YHWH babbled the language of all the earth...and scattered them"

The thrust of the episode is captured in its formal structure. The text begins neutrally, as a statement of fact, and closes with an explanation of the origin of linguistic and geographical diversity. Between these two poles is the action: man schemes with man as the action builds from earth to heaven; God responds, confers with his pantheon, and the action shifts back to the earth. At the outset, men talk to each other in one language; and at the end, no one understands his neighbor. In the opening geographical statement there is migration, settlement and common speech. The final notice is marked by a violent spatial dispersion correlated with the fracture of language and communication. The vessels of speech and space are shattered by human action. The text makes us painfully aware that speech binds lives and loosens them, builds society and isolates persons, and is both the crown and disgrace of our human existence.

The Tower of Babel episode is linked to the preceding narratives of the primeval cycle in several ways. First is the geographic setting: the "Tower" episode uses the geographical term *qedem*, "east," in its brief introduction. The descent of man "eastward" into history is once again signalized, as with Adam and Eve, and Cain.

The challenging act of mankind in Genesis 11:1–9 is to build a tower, a staged "mountain" "with its top in the heavens." In the beginning God placed Adam on a cosmic mountain, a world center of holiness and order. After the Flood, Noah, the new Adam, is given the blessings of a regenerated mankind on a mountain. Now man builds his own mountain, his monument of power and creaturely overreaching. In ancient Mesopotamia, temple towers called ziggurats and often described as having their "top in heaven" were symbolic of cosmic mountains and used as holy shrines.[16] Here the allusion to the building of such tower-mountains is used ironically, in a Mesopotamian setting, to express a deep ambivalence towards the works and achievements of civilization unmindful of its human limits. It also suggests a profound realization of the energies and will to self-deification which build culture ("city and tower"). A striking parallelism thus emerges between this episode on the aggressive motivations which underlie the tasks of culture and the earlier descriptions of Cain's descendants, who develop cities and art.

In fact, the achievements of culture are portrayed with sarcasm. Through their small deeds, brick by brick, men build a tower to the heavens so as to "make for ourselves a name." In the renewed world of labor and death and consciousness, man works to make a name for himself. Why? Only one answer seems plausible in this context and against the broader background of the cycle. Just as Adam left Eden without immortality, and just as the intercourse between the gods and women reintroduced immortality as a possibility (the results of the union were "men of name"!), so here the works of civilization are mocked as the way to find immortality. To make a "name" for oneself in the city (11:4) is man's doomed attempt to achieve symbolic immortality "east of Eden."[17] This is the same lesson which Gilgamesh learned after his failed quest for eternal life, though the "Gilgamesh" narrator conveys this lesson in tones less sarcastic and more resigned.

The human drive for social achievement is thus, from the perspective of Genesis 11:1–9, the drive to build a bulwark of "works" against the fear of death and dispersion. The resultant divine punishment, which counteracts this focused energy (cf. Genesis 3), reinforces the overall teaching of the primeval cycle: that man must learn his limits; that the unchecked expression of the drive for life is ultimately counterproductive and results in death, destruction, and isolation.

The irony of mankind's attempt to "make a name," to overreach itself and immortalize its achievements, is reinforced by the tightly coiled acoustical sound track of the text, which plays back the initial achievements as failures. Mankind goes eastward to build "there" *(sham)* a tower to the "heavens" *(sham-ayim)*, and so make a "name" *(shem)* for itself. It was "there" *(sham)* that human language was confounded, and it was "from there" *(mi-sham)* that mankind was scattered over the broad earth. In fact, the reversal of destiny in this paradigmatic presentation is signaled not only by these wordplays, but also by the symmetrical repetition of its many other words and word plays (cf. the diagram). Indeed, the very bricks *(li-be-na)* out of which the tower of human pretension is constructed are themselves symbolically deconstructed and reversed when God babbles *(na-bi-la)* the language of "all the earth" (v. 1) and scatters the builders "over all the earth" (v. 9).[18]

The primeval cycle ends after the genealogies of Shem (Semite) and Ever (Hebrew), with Abram. Universal history and its themes of will, wisdom, and death are concluded with the advent of a particular, national history, that of the fathers of the Israelite people. Several independent narratives have been fused by their common concerns so that the entire network of chapters reenergizes the whole. The unity of the cycle lies both in the coordinating and ever-progressive genealogies and in the repeated motifs, themes and symbols. The latter may be condensed as follows:

1. *Theme of Creation and Work*: "In the beginning"; after Eden; after the Flood; in the plains of Shinar.

2. *Symbolism of Sacred Space and the Mountain*: Eden; Ararat; the Tower.

3. *Man as gardener and "homo faber"* ("man the maker"): Adam; Cain; Noah; the neighbors of Shinar.

4. *Issue of Will, Desire, and Aggressive Rebellion*: Eve, Adam, and the serpent; the serpentine sin and Cain; the gods and the daughters of the earth; the builders of Babel.

5. *The Pantheon*: at the creation of man; at the exile from Eden; with the daughters of the earth; at the dispersal from Babel.

6. *Motif of Exile, Destruction, and Dispersion*: after the rebellion in Eden; after the murder of Abel; after the evil and violence in the generation of Noah; after the challenge of the builders of the Tower.

7. *Geographical Orientation*: the "garden of Eden away to the east"; the exile of man "east of Eden"; the exile of Cain "eastward of Eden": the movement of peoples "from the east" to build the Tower.

8. *Typology of Man and Time*: ten generations between Adam and Noah, who receives his blessing on a recreated earth; and ten generations from Noah to Abram.

Abram is, like Noah, a new Adam and a renewal of human life in history. In a sense, the entire primeval cycle is a prologue to him and his *toledot*. He is the new steward and hope "east of Eden." It is therefore striking, but by no means unexpected, that God's promises to him at the beginning of the patriarchal cycle (12:1–3) reverse the curses of Eden:

> And YHWH said to Abram: Leave your land, your birthplace, and your clan, and go to the land which I shall show you. I will make you into a great nation; I will bless you; and I will exalt your name, that you be for a blessing. I will bless those that bless you, and I will curse those that curse you; to the end that all the families of the earth will be blessed because of you.

Exile, curse, and the pain of childbirth "east of Eden" (cf. Genesis 3) now yield the hope of a new land and ingathering, of divine blessing, and of fertile generation. God will give Abram and his descendants an exalted "name" (cf. Genesis 6:4; 11:4); and the scattered multitudes, who have moved from God, will again have the opportunity to become a blessed family through Abram. By contrast to the frequent divine curses and reproaches found in the primeval cycle, the words of God in Genesis 12:1–3 are filled with hope and beneficence. The gloom of the preceding chapters is somewhat abated, and the possibility of earthly existence with God is renewed. With Abram and his faithful response to God's presence, the primeval cycle is brought to a close, and the cycle of the fathers begins.

3. Genesis 25:19-35:22/ The Jacob Cycle

The episodes of Jacob, his early life and trials, provide a rich context in which to study the patriarchal narratives in the Book of Genesis. Suppleness of style and structure, repetition of words and phrases, and techniques of disclosure and development are well blended and involve the reader in the unfolding of the text's meanings.

The episodes of Genesis 25:19–35:22 are composed of diverse genres and subjects: *toledot*-genealogies and birth notices, tales of Jacob and Esau in Canaan which frame others of Jacob and Laban in Aram, episodes of Isaac in Philistia and of Jacob's sons in Schechem, and encounters with divine beings at shrines and river fords.

What then is a suitable literary-interpretative approach to the illumination of all these elements? A focus on the textual boundaries of the Jacob Cycle provides an initial explication of the meaning of the text and a clue to the coordination of its subunits.

The Jacob Cycle is a series of episodes in the life of Jacob framed by the genealogical lists of the excluded sons, Ishmael and Esau. It is thus part of a larger patriarchal cycle of *toledot* in the Book of Genesis, linking the earlier "*toledot*-account of the creation of heaven and earth" and the ante- and postdiluvian genealogies with the list of Israelites opening the Book of Exodus (1:1-7).

The significance of this sequence of primeval *toledot* (Genesis 1-11) plus national *toledot* (Genesis 12-50) can be best appreciated against a broader background. Studies in the history of religion reveal that cultural teachings of origins often express a twofold concern.[1] The first type of teaching concerns the origin of the world and mankind, and includes episodes about the creation of the world, the formative events of human destiny (mortality, sex, wisdom), and the primordial forebears of human culture and their achievements. It thus focuses on the events of cosmic becoming and the universal nature of man. Genesis 1-11 provides such information in the Hebrew Bible.

A second type teaches the origins of the ancestors of the

nation. Such teachings are of immense significance for the orientation of a culture in time and space, providing accounts of the geographical origin of the group. They also offer both a history of the formative relationship of the people with certain provider-gods and a genealogical link to the origins of the people itself. Such teachings are to be found in Genesis 12–50, which constitute the collective *toledot* of how the Lord promised land, fertility, and blessing to Abram and his descendants. The Jacob Cycle, recorded in Genesis 25:19–35:22, deals with that patriarch's role in the total chain.[2]

Each of the fathers was a bearer of God's original promise to Abram (Genesis 12:1–3). It is referred to in 26:2 at the outset of Israel's adventures, and in 28:13–15, prior to Jacob's flight to Aram. Moreover, the promise is repeated at the end of each patriarch's life as well—e.g., in 22:17–18, after the last of Abraham's trials, the binding of Isaac; in 26:24, after Isaac's episode among the Philistines; and in 35:9–12, after Jacob's return to Canaan, his reconciliation with Esau, and the fulfillment of the vow made at the shrine of Beth-el years before (28:20–22). Such recapitulations give a religious stamp to each life cycle and, their mention at beginnings and ends, frame each of the patriarchal cycles with the hopes and fulfillments of divine promise. They all thus disclose a deep religious-literary coherence, despite the multiple traditions which they collectively represent.

Homeric scholarship provides a pertinent analogy for further insight into the coherence of the traditions found in the Jacob Cycle. Whereas earlier scholars of the past two centuries, most notably Wolff and Wilamowitz, displayed a solid skepticism regarding the unity and coherence of the *Iliad* and the *Odyssey*, the recent efforts of M. Parry have effected a shift in this perspective.[3] By studying the meter and epithets of both works, he has suggested that they reflect oral techniques of composition. These insights were supplemented by A. Lord on the basis of his research into the composition of Serbo-Croation epics, remarkably long recitations from diverse traditional building blocks.[4] The combined upshot of these works has been to restore respect for the techniques of composition and expansion in evidence in the Homeric epics. In a bold hypothesis, J. Myres has demonstrated the remarkable symmetry of the twenty-four books of the *Iliad*, and suggested that such symmetry reflects an editorial technique which had its conceptual origin in the bilateral symmetry of late Minoan pottery decoration.[5] More recently, C. Whitman has considerably deepened this insight, and showed that this symmetry is apparent not only among the books at set points in the twenty-four-book spectrum, but also within the subunits of these books.[6]

Such a technique of symmetry was noticed in the preceding analysis of the biblical Tower of Babel story. It is also the technique by which the diverse contents of the Jacob Cycle were integrated.

The Jacob Cycle, Genesis 25:19–35:22
(preceded by *toledot*)

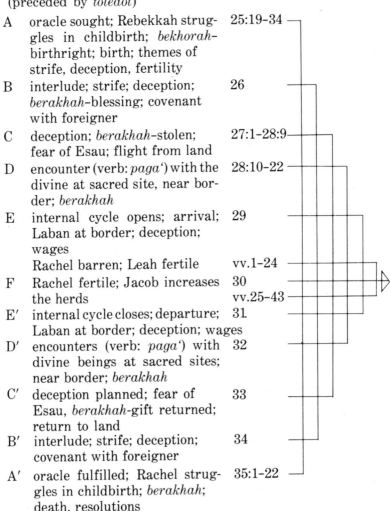

A	oracle sought; Rebekkah struggles in childbirth; *bekhorah*-birthright; birth; themes of strife, deception, fertility	25:19-34
B	interlude; strife; deception; *berakhah*-blessing; covenant with foreigner	26
C	deception; *berakhah*-stolen; fear of Esau; flight from land	27:1-28:9
D	encounter (verb: *paga'*) with the divine at sacred site, near border; *berakhah*	28:10-22
E	internal cycle opens; arrival; Laban at border; deception; wages	29
	Rachel barren; Leah fertile	vv.1-24
F	Rachel fertile; Jacob increases the herds	30
		vv.25-43
E'	internal cycle closes; departure; Laban at border; deception; wages	31
D'	encounters (verb: *paga'*) with divine beings at sacred sites; near border; *berakhah*	32
C'	deception planned; fear of Esau, *berakhah*-gift returned; return to land	33
B'	interlude; strife; deception; covenant with foreigner	34
A'	oracle fulfilled; Rachel struggles in childbirth; *berakhah*; death, resolutions	35:1-22

(succeeded by *toledot*)

The Jacob Cycle, part of the *toledot* of the still-living Isaac, begins with Rebekkah's pregnancy after many years of barrenness. During a difficult moment, Rebekkah consults a divine oracle which forecasts the birth of twins, the younger of whom would eventually prove superior. That younger twin is Jacob, who strives with his brother Esau repeatedly, eventually deceiving him into forfeiting his birthright as the eldest son. Soon thereafter, Jacob deceives Isaac as well, wresting from his father the patriarchal blessing. Jacob is "put up" to this last gambit by Rebekkah, who then advises him to flee Esau's wrath and go to Haran in Aram, where her relatives live. She induces Isaac, moreover, to bless that departure—which is to lead Jacob to the shrine of Beth-el, where he encounters the God of his fathers, and to Laban's home in Haran, where he indentures himself for Leah and Rachel. Rachel, his favorite, is initially barren and suffers shame before her fertile sister. However, soon after her own pregnancy, she and Jacob (and the rest of his family) leave Aram for Canaan, deceiving Laban en route. The return journey brings Jacob into encounters with divine beings and with his brother Esau, who, quite unexpectedly, receives him nobly. When Jacob returns home with his twelve sons (the last of whom, Benjamin, is born to Rachel, after entering Canaan), he fulfills the vow he had made years before at Beth-el, on his flight to Aram. The God of his fathers therewith confers upon him the national name "Israel"—a name first bestowed after his successful encounter with a divine being at the Jabbok ford on his return to Canaan. The cycle is followed by references to Jacob's sons, although reference to events in the lives of Simon and Levi does occur within the cycle itself.

Presented below is a closer literary analysis of this recapitulation of the scenario of the Jacob Cycle. Following the preceding design, Genesis 25:19–34 is paired with Genesis 35:1–22, Genesis 26 with Genesis 34, and so on.

Genesis 25:19-34 (A) and Genesis 35:1-22 (A′)*

Genesis 25:19-34 (A) is a short, highly compressed composition which introduces the cycle as a whole. Its contents set the scene for the life of the patriarch Jacob and foreshadow subsequent narrative developments.

---

*The letters "A" and "A¹," "B" and "B¹," "C" and "C¹" refer the reader back to the pairings of the diagram on page 42.

These are the *toledot* of Isaac, son of Abraham. Abraham had sired Isaac. Now Isaac was forty years old when he married Rebekkah, the daughter of Bethuel the Aramean of Padan Aram, [and] the sister of Laban the Aramean. Isaac entreated [*wayye'tar*] YHWH for his wife because she was barren; and YHWH was entreated by his plea [*wayye'ater*], and Rebekkah his wife conceived. But the sons so struggled within her, that she said: "If so be it, why should I live?" She then went to consult YHWH [by oracle]. YHWH said to her:

> "There are two nations in your womb,
> So that two peoples will emerge from your thighs;
> One people will be stronger than the other,
> And the elder will serve the younger."

When her period of pregnancy was terminated, indeed there were twins in her womb. The first emerged ruddy, covered with hair [*se'ar*] like a hairy mantle; so they called him Esau. Next emerged his brother, holding the heel ['*aqev*] of Esau; so they called him Jacob [*ya'aqov*]. Isaac was sixty years old when she bore them.

As the boys grew older Esau became a skilled hunter, a man of the field; while Jacob became a simple man, a tent-dweller. So Isaac had love-preference for Esau because he liked the taste of game; but Rebekkah loved Jacob. Upon a time, when Jacob was cooking lentils, Esau returned exhausted from the field. Esau said to Jacob: "Give me a gulp of red curd ['*adom*], for I am exhausted." (Therefore he was called '*Edom.*) But Jacob said, "First sell me your birthright [*bekhorah*]." Esau said: "I am half dead so what do I need a birthright for?" Thereupon Jacob said, "Swear to me on the spot." So he swore to him, and sold his birthright to Jacob. Then Jacob gave Esau bread and lentils, who ate, drank, rose, and left. Thus did Esau despise his birthright.

This prologue hints at themes and issues which recur in the Jacob narrative and thereby provides it with cohesion and tension. The oracle cited above—that of Jacob's ultimate superiority—is the principal foreshadowing statement of the prologue. However, three instances of anticipation appear before it. The first is the brief reference to Rebekkah as both daughter of Bethuel and sister of Laban, who lives in Padan Aram (v.20). These relationships and this location will be reevoked when Jacob's mother Rebekkah urges him to flee to her brother Laban in Aram after his deception of Esau (27:43). He will there negotiate with Laban for Rachel. The second instance involves Rebekkah's being barren (*'aqarah*, v. 21) before the birth of Jacob. The fact that Jacob's wife Rachel is also initially barren (*'aqarah*, 29:31) will be dramatically significant in the later narrative. The third case of foreshadowing is the reference to Rebekkah's difficult pregnancy, "when the sons struggled within her." This feature of struggle and strife is the recurrent thematic emblem of the cycle as a whole: the brothers struggle in the womb (25:22), at birth (25:26), and in their youth (25:27-34); Jacob later struggles with Laban (Genesis 29-31), Rachel "strives" with Leah (cf. 30:8), and Jacob wrestles with a divine being (32:25-31). Thus the prologue sets the tone for the dominant motif of *agon*, or struggle, which affects all the characters.

As was noted, these elements precede the divine oracle to Rebekkah (v.23). They provoke anticipations in the reader and generate the flow of the narrative. The oracle itself, which announces that "the elder will serve the younger," creates maximal tension by its preview of the outcome. For the oracle raises for the reader the wonderment as to how Jacob will succeed and how the divine promises will be fulfilled through human actions.

In the oracle, Jacob is called the "younger" *(tza'ir)* brother, and Esau is called the "elder" *(rav)*, brother. This fraternal contrast is also significant, for it anticipates the parallel strife between the sisters Rachel and Leah, the first called the "younger" *(tze'irah)* and the second called the "firstborn" *(bekhirah)* in 29:26. Rachel ultimately prevails over her elder sister, as has her husband Jacob over his brother.

The oracle serves another significant function. It provides Rebekkah with the foreknowledge that her younger son will prevail, thus clarifying her motivation in the deception of Isaac, and mitigating its apparent immorality.

A final anticipatory element in the prologue is suggested by a significant omission, or asymmetry, in the popular etymologies provided for Esau and Jacob. It will be noted that whereas two etymologies exist for the name "Esau" only one is provided for the name "Jacob." In v.25, the elder brother is born ruddy *('admoni)* and hairy, "like a hairy mantle." But he is named "Esau" here and not yet "Edom," as would have been more appropriate for the "explanation" given. A second folk-etymology for him follows in v.30. During adolescence, Esau sells his birthright to Jacob for a lump of red lentils *('adom)* and therefore, the text states, he is called "Edom."

Jacob *(ya'aqov)* is so called because he was born holding the heel *('eqev)* of his twin brother (v.26). This etymology appears with and balances the birth etymology of Esau (v.25). But no second etymology for Jacob balances the second etymology for Esau in v.30. Such a second etymology does occur, later however, in Genesis 27:36, where it serves to underpin Jacob's second deception of his brother. The first deception scenario and etymology for the name "Jacob" in chapter 25 thus anticipate the second in chapter 27.

As seen from the condensed language and images of this prologue, the Jacob Cycle opens as a tale of barrenness and birth, of deception and strife, of rights and priorities, and of blessing and power. As intimated, these issues recur throughout the narrative. They will be traced below.

The multiple tensions ebb only in *Genesis 35 (A')*, the denouement of the Cycle. This chapter brings all matters to a final resolution and concludes the *toledot* of Isaac. Jacob returns to Beth-el (v.1), where he first received the patriarchal promise when he fled from his brother Esau (Genesis 28). He had then vowed to build an altar to the Lord in Beth-el, should he survive his ordeal and return to Canaan. Once the tensions with Esau are relieved in chapter 33, Jacob returns to his homeland and fulfills his vow (35:7). At the conclusion, at Bethel, just as earlier, Jacob receives the patriarchal blessing (35:11-12) and the name "Israel" (35:16), a name first given after his night encounter with a divine being (32:29). Rachel dies at the conclusion of this Cycle, and the *toledot* of Jacob, through his sons, begins (vv.23-26.).

Genesis 26(B) and Genesis 34(B')

The very presence in the Jacob Cycle of *Genesis 26 (B)*— which narrates episodes between Isaac and the Philistine king of Gerar and subsequent squabbles between their respective shepherds—raises several questions. Is it not anomalous in the present context, after the prologue of Jacob and Esau in 25:19-34 and before Jacob's deception of Isaac and flight from Esau in 27:1-28:9? Can the textual interruption be sufficiently explained as a time-filler between the youth and early manhood of Jacob?

It must be noted that the symmetrical episode (see diagram, p. 42) in *Genesis 34 (B')* is also without visible relationship to its surrounding context. It has nothing to do either with the preceding reconciliation between Jacob and Esau (Genesis 33) or with the succeeding return to Beth-el (Genesis 35:1-22). Its scenario concerns an event in the life of Jacob's sons, Simeon and Levi, who avenged the rape of their sister Dinah through a deception of the culprit people of Shechem. The events in the lives of Jacob's sons are otherwise reported after the close of the Cycle. In a narrative ensemble whose whole thrust and delight revolves around the character Jacob as striver, deceiver, and hero, the focus on his sons in chapter 34 is as unexpected as was the focus on his father in chapter 26. Quite certainly, then, Genesis 26 serves as an interlude between the opening oracle of strife and tension and its fulfillment. And Genesis 34 serves as an interlude bridging Jacob's reconciliation with Esau and the denouement at Beth-el.

Without chapter 26, Genesis 25 and 27 would be more harmoniously joined. This point follows not only from thematic considerations, but is also supported by the fact, noted above, that the second name-etymology of Jacob is given in 27:36, where Esau calls him Jacob *(ya'aqov)* "because he has deceived me *[ye'aqveniy]* twice." In a parallel manner Genesis 34 interrupts Genesis 33 and 35. The events of the sons of Jacob in Shechem are secondary to the main narrative line: Jacob's reconciliation with Esau, and his return to Beth-el in Canaan.

The symmetry between Genesis 26 and 34, together with their parallel functions as interludes, thus preclude any assumption of a haphazard editorial arrangement. Moreover, they are linked to each other and to their respective contexts by the common themes of deception and strife. The first section of chapter 26, in which Isaac deceives Abimelekh with regard to Rebekkah (v.7), involves a case of strife wherein a wife is called a "sister" *('ahot)* and there is fear of intercourse (stem: *shakhav)* with a member of an uncircumcised ethnic group. In its second section, in which Isaac charges the Philistines with deception (v.27), there is a case of strife among the shepherds (v.20) as well as an issue of covenantal malfeasance in which the treaty partners are called "brothers" *('ahim)*. In a parallel way, Genesis 34 also reports an event involving deception *(mirmah,* v.34; cf. 27:35; and 29:25)—but now because of an actual case of intercourse (stem: *shakhav)* between the "uncircumcised" Schechem ben Hamor and Dinah, the sister *('ahot)* of Simeon and Levi. The deception also involves covenantal malfeasance (v.10) and considerable strife.

While the interludes in chapters 26 and 34 divert the pace of the Jacob Cycle, they also enlarge our sense of the lives of the patriarchs. From the outset the issues of entangling relations and marital complexity are expressed. The interludes, while suspending the main action, mirror these issues along a broader familial continuum. They are witnesses to the creative-artistic imagination which synthesized the multiple traditions of the Jacob Cycle as a whole.

Genesis 27:1-28:9 (C) and Genesis 33 (C′)

The next unit in the narrative begins with *Genesis 27:1* and continues to *Genesis 28:9 (C)*. While this subdivision overlaps the chapter division, it has unity of both theme and focus. The paragraphing of traditional Rabbinic Bibles confirms this division: Genesis 28:9 is signaled as a major disjuncture; after it, at 28:10, there begins a new *parashah* or lectionary unit. The common chapter and verse division, which here differs from the *parashah* division, is a later product stemming from the Christian Middle Ages.

Genesis 28:1-9 deals with the theme of flight following Jacob's deception of Esau, and is thereby apparently linked to the preceding chapter 27. But this surface solution is insufficient; the matter is more complicated. For it has long been noted by modern biblical criticism that these two passages (27 and 28:1-9) reveal a contradictory set of motives for Jacob's departure. In the first case the blessing is taken by stealth and the culprit is urged to flee; in the second, Isaac gives Jacob a blessing and advises him not to choose a bride from the local population, but to return to Aram and there find a wife.

Although this apparent discrepancy reflects an example of multiple sources, the present integration of the chapters must also be considered. The following solution is therefore offered. After Rebekkah counsels Jacob to flee, she goes to Isaac and wails (v.46):

> My life will be shortened because of these Hittite women: should Jacob marry one of the Hittite women, like these natives, what do I have to live for?

These words were undoubtedly meant to recall to Isaac the breach of endogamy effected by Esau in 26:34 and his reaction in v.35.

And Esau was forty years old when he married Yehudith, daughter of Be'eri, the Hittite, and Basmath, daughter of Eylon, the Hittite, Isaac and Rebekkah became deeply embittered.

The effect was that Isaac summoned Jacob, counseled him to leave and marry among his kinsmen, and blessed him. Accordingly, Rebekkah's supplication of Isaac in 27:46 to preserve endogamy transforms the motivation in 28:1-9 for Jacob's departure from one in flat contradiction to 27:41-45 (fear of Esau's revenge) to one supplementary to it. Moreover, just as Rebekkah's first act of deceit in 27:5-13 is tempered by our awareness of her knowledge of the oracle, so now the brunt of her second act of deceit (of Isaac) is tempered by her presented concern for an unsullied lineage. At all events, Genesis 28:1-9 certainly concludes the unit of events in Canaan beginning in 27:1; for with 28:10, "Jacob left Beersheva and journeyed to Haran."

Genesis 27:1-45 comes to expression through its words and speeches, which provide the text's dynamic and structure. Numerous voices surface and are given play: true voices and false ones, conniving voices and blessings, shrewd voices and pained cries. The depth of the deception is conveyed by the fact that people speak their own words and those of others. The interweaving of the words and repetitions creates the text's tension of appearance and reality, power and possibility. The following outline provides a visual sense of this.

a   Isaac and Esau. *Scenario opens*

b   Rebekkah and Jacob, *Advice*: "Listen to me"

c   Jacob and Isaac, *Deception and Blessing*

c' Esau and Isaac, *Torment and Blessing*

b' Rebekkah and Jacob, *Advice*: "Listen to me"

a' Rebekkah and Isaac, *Scenario closes*

The preceding diagram, like that observed for the Cycle as a whole, is symmetrical. Between the opening frame *(a)* which generates the action, and the closing one *(a')* which connects it with 28:1-9, are Rebekkah's deceptions and ploys *(b / b')*. Here

the central action of the text takes shape: Jacob's deception of
Isaac, and Esau's attempt to wrest "one (little) blessing" from
his father. Isaac's blessing of Jacob and Essau stands at the
center of the text *(c/c')*, and provides the linchpin for its
various speeches, stratagems, hopes, and fears. Finally, this
diagram reveals what Olrik called a "law" of epic composition, namely the convention of "two to a scene."[7] Through this
fairly universal technique, epic narratives isolate the focus on
one pair of characters in any one scene and thereby modulate
narrative tensions and information.

On the basis of the foregoing diagram, one can perceive
another dimension of the text: repeated speeches by one or two
characters at different points in the narrative, repetitions
which have the effect of giving dramatic focus to the dissem-
bling, injustice, and irony that pervade the text. Thus Rebekkah
begins her counsels to Jacob prior to both the first and second
deceptions of Isaac with the phrase "Listen to me" (*b* and *b'*,
vv.8,43). The repetition underscores Rebekkah's aggressive
manipulations and Jacob's passive complicity. By the same
token, the pathos of the masquerade and deception is fully
underscored in *c* and *c'* where both Jacob and Esau speak
similar words of introduction to Isaac. Thus in vv.18-19 *(c)*
Jacob says: "'My father!,' and he said: 'Who are you, my son?'
And Jacob said to his father: 'I am Esau your firstborn.'"
These words recur in vv.31-32 *(c')*, where Esau says: "'Let my
father arise and eat.... And Isaac his father said to him: 'Who
are you?' and he said: 'I am Esau your firstborn son.'" The
irony of this second dialogue is most painful.

In addition to these two instances of dual repetition of a
speech, there is also a case of quadruple repetition. The words
spoken by Isaac to Esau in vv.3-4, regarding hunting game
and serving it up to him on his deathbed, so that he could bless
him before his death, are repeated by the eavesdropping
Rebekkah to Jacob in v.6, by the deceiving Jacob to Isaac in
v.19, and by the wronged Esau to Isaac in v.31. This repetition
of the original motivation-speech in the mouth of the various
characters gives ironic continuity to the narrative and counterpoints the successive developments.

An analysis of key words in Genesis 27 reveals the power
struggle for the blessing which undergirds the family drama.
The verbal stem *barekh* ("bless"), to which the noun *berakhah*
("blessing") and the past participle *barukh* ("blessed") are
related, recurs some twenty-two times in Genesis 27:1-28:9.

The deception for the blessing-*berakhah* in chapter 27 is linked to and completes the first deception, for the birthright-*bekhorah*, in chapter 25.

Other key words have a decisive presence in this text as well. The recurrent use of the term *'ah* ("brother") underscores the centrality of the fraternal element in Genesis 27:1–28:9: Jacob and Esau are brothers; Isaac refers to Jacob as Esau's brother; and Rebekkah tells Jacob to flee to her brother Laban until the wrath of his brother Esau is assuaged. Similarly, the key word *qol* ("voice") underpins the dynamics of the chapter. At the outset, Rebekkah, "overhearing" Isaac's instructions to Esau, says to Jacob: "Now, my son, listen to my voice" (v.8). She repeats this command twice more, once in v.13 to egg on the balking Jacob, and again in v.43, when she tries to instigate his flight for fear of Esau's reprisals. This emphasis on the *qol* is especially significant in a text whose pathos centers around Isaac's poor vision. Accordingly, the action of the text focuses less on visual images than on the senses of smelling, feeling, and hearing. These latter combine at the dramatic center of the text. When Jacob deceives Isaac, the latter smells and feels Jacob, and then remarks: "the voice *[qol]* is the voice *[qol]* of Jacob, but the hands are the hands of Esau."

One final term should be mentioned in this regard, both because of its dramatic significance to this text and because of its recurrence later on. In v.12 Jacob is described as smooth-skinned; he consequently fears that his father will "feel" him (stem: *mashash*) when he approaches, and so discover his duplicity. Although Isaac did "feel" him (vv.21–22), he was nonetheless duped. Years later, in an ironic reversal, Jacob's wife Rachel (the younger sibling) stole the household gods—perhaps symbolic of inheritance rights[8]—from her own father Laban, who "felt" (stem: *mashash*) her baggage in search of them (31:34, 37). The search was inconclusive, and a patriarchal blessing was again abducted deceitfully.

Genesis 33 (C') describes the reconciliation between Jacob and Esau. This event is Jacob's first act upon returning to Canaan, and balances the deception and flight of Genesis 27:1–28:9. It bristles with ironic overtones. Since Jacob cannot know whether Esau's anger has subsided during the years of their separation, he is both cautious and wily. He anticipates the encounter with fear and plots a stratagem "to propitiate" Esau. When they do finally meet, Jacob offers his brother a gift, saying: "Take my *berakhah* which has been brought to you" (33:11). The pun is stunning. Before the encounter, by way of preparation, Jacob has planned to appease Esau by offering him wealth. Speaking to his subordinates, Jacob has called the gift a *minhah*, the proper term for such a tribute-offering. But the guilt of his wealth, gotten through the beneficence of a stolen blessing, lies heavily upon his tongue. So, when he turns to Esau, he not only says, "take my *minhah* (v.10), but also: "take my *berakhah*" (v.11).

By this unconscious double-entendre (*berakhah* can occasionally mean "gift," as in Judges 1:15), Jacob confesses his guilt and verbalizes his inner conflicts. What he says, in effect, is "Take [back] the blessing which I have tricked from you." Esau does, in fact, accept it from Jacob. By such an external transaction the internal guilt of a misappropriated blessing is "atoned" for. This latter point is also made by a pun; for while the verbal stem *kapper* in Jacob's earlier instructions (32:21), "I shall *kapper* him with a *minhah*," means "propitiate," it equally suggests the meaning "atone." The guilt and appeasement dimension of this fraternal meeting is further underscored by the fact that just before Jacob makes his verbal slip in v.11, and says "take my *berakhah*," he said: "if I have found favor with you, take my *minhah* from me...and forgive me."

Having come to terms with Esau (chap. 33, Jacob returns to Beth-el and receives the "national name" of "Israel" (35:10). But, to be sure, Jacob had received this name earlier, after his successful encounter with a divine being on his return to Canaan (32:29). The net effect of the repeated bestowal of the national name is to suggest that only after Jacob's reconciliation with his brother Esau is he truly the patriarchal heir "Israel." This point is subtly effected in the text through key words. In Genesis 32:30, after his encounter with a divine being, it is said that Jacob "saw God face to face." On the morrow, during his reconciliation with Esau, Jacob implores his brother to accept the proffered gift, "for I have seen your face which ·is like seeing the face of God" (33:10). From a psychological viewpoint, the juxtaposition and verbal splicing of the wrestling and reconciliation scenes (chaps. 32 and 33) suggest that Jacob's night strife may be understood as a figurative preparation for his morning encounter with Esau.

The wrestling scene thus appears to be part of Jacob's dream-work, whereby he "works through" the anticipated struggle with Esau by fusing it with earlier wrestlings with his brother—in the womb and at birth. The use of the wrestling image not only underscores the *agon*-struggle which Jacob anticipates with Esau, but effectively discloses the psychic core of the event (also indicated by the tongue-slip). Compounded by guilt, the anticipated fraternal strife is fused with an earlier one, allowing Jacob to resolve the conflict raging within him. In the "night encounter" Jacob wrestles with the "Esau" he carried within him. The "rebirth" Jacob achieves by his psychic victory in the night had still to be confirmed in the light of day. Jacob awakens with the deep conviction that he had faced his struggle with courage and had been blessed by divinity. He greets the morning light with the glow of his own self-transformation and illumination. Having seen Elohim face to face at Penuel, Jacob can prepare to meet Esau face to face as well.

Genesis 28:10–22 (D) and Genesis 32 (D′)

In *Genesis 28:10–22 (D)*, Jacob fled from his brother Esau and "encounters" (v.11, stem: *paga*ʻ) the border shrine of Bethel, where he beheld divine beings—*malʼakei ʼelohim*—"rising and descending" a stairway. The symbolism and descriptive imagery of this ascension-vision has been manifestly derived from the visual appearance and religious function of ancient Mesopotamian temple-towers. These shrines are known to have had stairways leading to the summit where divine beings communicated with mortals; and they are often described as having their "top in heaven." It is thus a striking feature of the narrator's description of Jacob's vision, just prior to his return to northern Mesopotamia, that he has the patriarch perceive a "stairway...set on the ground, with its top in the heavens."[9] This and more; for it is there that Jacob encounters YHWH, the God of his fathers, and is promised his fathers' blessing. He, in turn, vows to worship YHWH and build Him a shrine should he return to Canaan in safety. This vow is, in fact, fulfilled by Jacob at Beth-el upon his return (35:7).

The thematic counterpoint to this episode is *Genesis 32 (D′)*. On his way out of Padan Aran, in flight from his "brother" Laban (so called in 29:15!), "Jacob went on his way and encountered (verb: *paga*ʻ) divine beings *[malʼakhei ʼelohim]*." The place of this encounter was at the border shrine Mahanayim, so called because divine beings were "encamped" there. Several verbal and thematic contacts thus occur between *D* and *D'*, which bracket the tale-within-the-tale in the land of Aram.

Mal'akh ("messenger," "angel") is a theme word in chapter 32. Immediately after the aforementioned encounter with divine *mal'akhim* ("messengers") at Mahanayim, Jacob sent human *mal'akhim* to his brother Esau. Further, the entire unit concludes with Jacob *(ya'aqov)* wrestling *('avaq)* with a "man" at the Jabbok *(yavoq)* ford, a text discussed above. Seeing this being, it is said, was like seeing "Elohim face to face." This "man" is, then, portrayed as a divine agent—a point confirmed by Hosea 12. In Hosea, Jacob is said to have struggled with Elohim (God/"divine powers") and a *mal'akh* ("messenger"):

> In his might he struggled with Elohim;
> He struggled with the *mal'akh* and prevailed (vv.4a–5b).

This couplet parallels Genesis 32:29, where Jacob is named "Israel," because "you have struggled with Elohim and man and prevailed."

Genesis 32 is thus structured around the term *mal'akh*:

I. Genesis 32:2-3   Jacob encounters *mal'akhei 'elohim* at a sacred site.
II. Genesis 32:3-24   Jacob sends *mal'akhim* to Esau.
III. Genesis 32:25-33 Jacob wrestles with an *'ish/mal'akh* at a sacred site.

The two encounters with divine beings/agents-*mal'akhim* (I and III) frame the dispatch of human *mal'akhim*-messengers to Esau (II). Because of this structure it seems preferable to join 32:1-3 with the rest of chapter 32 rather than the preceding Laban materials, as was done by ancient Rabbinic tradition.

In conclusion, it is worth reemphasizing that *D* and *D'* are thematically balanced through encounters by Jacob with divine beings at border shrines (Genesis 28:10ff./32:25-33). The first occasion is on his flight out of the land, the second is on his way in. These strivings of Jacob complement others during his long life, including the many struggles with Laban in the land of Aram (chaps. 29-31). Indeed, the entire Jacob Cycle might well be dubbed *Jacob Agonistes*, for it contains his many struggles to establish himself in the world. The life trials of Jacob are less manifestly theological than those of Abraham because he is tested more by his responses to daily turmoil. In the end he proves worthy to be an ancestor of his people by his ability to withstand difficulties. He is Jacob the "overcomer," the "prevailer" renamed "Israel."

Genesis 29(E) and Genesis 31(E')

The divine encounters in Genesis 28:10ff., during Jacob's flight from Canaan, and in chapter 32, upon his return, frame what Gunkel considered to be the original Jacob–Laban saga, around whose nucleus diverse traditions accumulated. Gunkel was led to this conclusion insofar as chapters 29–31 include distinctly different issues and are set in a locale different from that of the chapters which now frame it. Its present function is that of a tale-within-the-tale, focusing on Jacob's life in Aram after his flight from Esau. Like the frame-narrative, Genesis 29–31 is a tale of strife between "brother" (nephew) and "brother" (uncle); but it is also a tale of strife between sister and sister, and between sister and father. And like the frame-narrative, Genesis 29–31 is also rife with the themes of barrenness and fertility, of recrimination and deceit.

Genesis 29–31 thus counterpoint the surrounding tale of Esau. Indeed, on reading *Genesis 29 (E)*, one has the distinct sense of déjà vu. The *agon* of Jacob in pursuit of Rachel, of Rachel in contest with Leah, of Jacob deceived by Laban, and of Laban deceived by Rachel: all mirror the preceding strife between Jacob and Esau and the former's deception of Isaac. By such a foil, moreover, the final formulator of the cycle gives Jacob his comeuppance and circumspectly redresses the injustice of his original act of deceit (in Genesis 27). When Jacob fulfills the serf tenure which Laban has demanded (apparently as a bride-price) for Rachel, but is given Leah in her stead, he reproaches Laban, "his brother": "Why have you deceived me [stem: *rimmah*, 29:25]?" To which Laban rejoins (v.26): "It is not our [local] custom to marry off the younger [*tze'irah*] before the firstborn [*bekhirah*]." The counterpoint with Genesis 27 is obvious: there Jacob was the younger *(tza'ir/qaton)* who misappropriated the birthright *(bekhorah)* of his elder brother *(rav/gadol)* by deception (stem: *rimmah*, 27:35). With his indignant protest to Laban, Jacob unwittingly condemns himself.

The incident of deception found in *Genesis 29(E)*, during Jacob's early settlement in Aram, is balanced by those presented in *Genesis 31(E')*, on the occasion of Jacob's and Rachel's departure for Canaan. Not only does Jacob refer to

Laban's earlier deceits (stem: *talal*; v.7), but the departure is itself redolent with new acts of deceit, underscored by the dense repetition of the verbal stem *ganav*, "to steal," in its several nuances. Rachel "stole" the household gods from her father (v.19) and deceives him when he catches up with her to inspect her baggage (v.35); Laban asks Jacob why he has twice "stolen my heart" (v.26) and acted "deceitfully" (v.28); and Jacob, accused by Laban of "stealing" his household gods (v.30), remarks that he left in flight since he feared Laban would accuse him of "kidnapping" his two daughters (stem: *gazal*, v.31). Jacob further maintained that he never "stole" anything (v.39) from Laban during his long tenure in Aram (v.39)—"for he did not know" that Rachel had "stolen" her father's household gods.

The counterpoints between Genesis 27 and 31 are like those between 27 and 29, thematic and verbal. Both Jacob and Rachel deceive their fathers and flee from home. Rachel deceives Laban by misappropriating his household gods, which represent the patriarchal blessing and inheritance. She also lies to him when, having caught up to her, he "felt" (stem: *mashash*; vv.34,37) for them like a blind man. It will be recalled that precisely the same verb is used in 27:22, when Isaac felt Jacob's hands during the latter's attempt to misappropriate the patriarchal blessing.

Genesis 29 (E) and *31 (E')* thus provide a thematic counterpoint to the main narrative. In Aram as in Canaan there is deception, stealth, and strife: between brother and brother, sister and sister, and sister and father. At the center of all this mendacity is Jacob's pursuit of Rachel. She is the object of his trials. But she is barren. And, indeed, this issue of Rachel's barrenness and fertility in Genesis 30 is the thematic watershed of the entire Cycle.

Genesis 30(F)

Genesis 30, which stands at the center of the Jacob Cycle, is composed of two units:

A   Genesis 30:1-24   Rachel is barren and conceives
B   Genesis 30:25-43   Jacob determines to leave Aram
                         and expands his herd

This subdivision can be more fully appreciated through a consideration of the first and last verses of each unit:

A Genesis 30:1-24

vv.1-2   "When Rachel saw that she could not bear children for Jacob, Rachel was jealous of her sister. She said to Jacob: 'Give me children, else I'll die.'"

vv.22-23   "Then Elohim remembered Rachel; and Elohim responded and opened her womb. So she conceived and bore a son, and said, 'Elohim has removed my shame.'" (In v.24 she names the son Joseph.)

The text opens with a notice of Rachel's barrenness and resentment of her sister. Out of frustration, she demanded children from Jacob. The unit concludes with a report of divine grace, Rachel's conception, and her delivery of a son. Within this literary framework is the full measure of Rachel's turmoil, shame, and desperation.

The strife between Rachel and Leah is summed up in one poignant remark by Rachel, given as the etymology for the name "Naphtali," Jacob's son through her concubine Bilhah: "I have struggled mightily *[naphtuley 'elohim]* with my sister and have prevailed" (v.8). With this expression, Rachel's situation ironically recalls that of her husband Jacob, who "strove with Elohim and man and prevailed." But there is a further irony. In the despair of her barrenness, Rachel hired out Jacob (stem: *sakhar*) to Leah in exchange for the latter's fertility charm (vv.14-16), an act which contrasts the fact that Jacob was himself a hireling (stem: *sakhar*) of Laban for the sake of Rachel (Genesis 29:15; cf. 30:28; 31:7-8,41).

At the core of Rachel's strife with Leah, then, is the issue of fertility. The second unit of chapter 30 makes this particularly clear.

B Genesis 30:25-43

v.25   "And it was when Rachel had given birth to Joseph, Jacob said to Laban: 'Let me now return to my homeland.'"

v.43   "So the man [Jacob] became exceedingly wealthy, possessing many flocks, and also maidservants, manservants, camels, and donkeys."

Verse 25 provides the thematic and structural pivot of the Cycle: As soon as Rachel gives birth, Jacob plans his return home. The continuity of the line of Abraham and Isaac is therewith assured through Jacob's favorite wife; and a reversal in spatial and interpersonal action now follows. This denouement is dramatized in chapters 31–35, already reviewed, whose traditions are so integrated as to provide an overall balance to the entire narrative. The Jacob Cycle thus emerges as a sustained work of literary imagination. It is the *toledot*—in the fullness of its hopes and strife, trials and blessings—of Jacob, who becomes "Israel."

It remains to be inquired whether the preceding structural analysis of Genesis 25:19–35:22 can shed any light on the structure and composition of other biblical narratives. To follow through on this, several recent developments in folktale analysis must be brought into view. Until fairly recently, the study of folktales had been largely concerned with uncovering the core motif of a tale and then showing how this was modified or expanded in different cultural matrices. Gunkel's search for the root of the Jacob Cycle in the "Einzelsage" (core saga) of the Jacob–Laban scenario reflects the impact of these interests in biblical literary criticism.[10] However, a methodological revision in folklore studies has shifted the analytical focus to more holistic considerations. Such a view considers a tale or narrative less from a linear perspective, whereby the separate parts are isolated and their development "explained," and more from the integrative consideration of a narrative as a seamless web of interanimating components. The first viewpoint is commonly called diachronic, the second synchronic.[11]

In his seminal structural analysis of Russian folktales, Vladimir Propp suggested that the minimal folk-unit should be expanded from core motifs to action sequences.[12] He demonstrated that the components of certain action sequences remain remarkably stable in diverse tales *even though* the specific depiction of the actions and characters might vary. Thus, for example, the action sequence of a hero who is given beneficent magical powers by a mysterious donor, and is then persecuted by a villain but survives, is common in Russian folktales, although the depiction of the hero, the magical device, the donor, or the villain may vary. A determinate number of action sequences may thus be realized in an indeterminate number of ways.

Propp made certain universal claims for oral folk literature. While it is beyond the scope of the present study to test the validity of these claims for the Bible—whose literature is, in any case, a *literary* (not oral) deposit—his principle of action sequences does illumine the structure of several narrative tableaux and compositional techniques found in the Jacob Cycle and elsewhere in biblical literature. Several of these now follow.

1. The Jacob Cycle opens (25:19ff.) with an action-sequence which depicts a barren woman who, in her plight, goes to a divine oracle and is promised children. This sequence has several variations elsewhere in Scripture. In Genesis 18, Sarah is barren. Divine messengers come to Abraham, who serves them a meal near a tree, and they give an oracular pronouncement that Sarah will conceive and bear within the year. Similarly, in Judges 13, the wife of Manoah is barren. The future father of Samson is visited by a divine messenger who gives a birth oracle for the upcoming year. Manoah serves the messenger a meal and inquires after his name. The messenger refuses and ascends to heaven in a flame.

More partial residues of these components are evidenced by Judges 6 and Samuel 1. In the first case a divine messenger comes to Gideon with an oracle of confidence. The messenger is served a meal near a tree, but refuses to divulge his name and ascends to heaven in smoke. In the second instance, Hannah is barren, goes to a shrine on a festival, and there receives a birth oracle for the upcoming year.[13]

2. As seen, the Jacob Cycle opens with a prologue—the promise of Jacob's ascendancy over his older brother—which foreshadows the themes and dynamics of the entire narrative ensemble. Similar proleptic devices may be found in other narrative units. In Genesis 12:1–3, the promise of land, seed and blessing opens and reappears at significant dramatic intervals throughout the patriarchal cycle (chapters 12–50). In Genesis 37, the oracle dreams of Joseph anticipate the developments and interpersonal dynamics of the entire cycle of Joseph, his brothers, and their father Jacob (chapters 37–50). In Judges 13, the birth oracle with its Nazirite-type prohibitions—which is disclosed to Manoah—ironically counterpoints the abrogation of the latter by Samson in the succeeding narrative (chapters 14–16). And in Exodus 3:7ff., the oracle-promise of national deliverance given to Moses finds its fulfillment through the course of the Book of Exodus (chapters 3–19).

3. Related to the preceding foreshadowing techniques is

another which recurs in Genesis 25:19-35:22. It was noted that chapters 26 and 34 were interludes interrupting the main narrative. In the first case, the interlude followed the opening prologue and delayed its fulfillment. A similar feature can be noted in Genesis 38, which comes between the dream oracles of chapter 37 and their fulfillment in 39ff. That the Judah-Tamar incident is intrusive within the Joseph narrative is suggested both by its overall independent theme and by the absence of Joseph from its venue. The independence of Genesis 38 is also structurally indicated by the fact that the last verse of chapter 37 is repeated when the narrative thread is resumed in the first verse of Genesis 39.

The preceding analysis of structures of biblical narrative composition has focused on the surface layer of textual discourse. This horizontal view can be complemented by a vertical one which attempts to disclose dialectical tensions operative beneath the surface of the text.[14]

Three issues are of primary importance in Genesis 25:19-35:22: *birth*, *blessing*, and *land*. These correspond, as will be recalled, to the threefold patriarchal blessing given to Abraham (12:1-3). The first of these issues is the concern for *birth*. It first surfaces with Rebekkah's barrenness, her difficult pregnancy, and the birth of Jacob and Esau; and it appears as well with Rachel, who is initially barren, and spends her early years in preoccupied agony over her failure to conceive and give birth. The second is that of *blessing*: God blesses Isaac in Philistia; Jacob steals Isaac's blessing, Isaac blesses both brothers, Jacob is blessed by a divine messenger at Penuel; and God blesses Jacob at Beth-el. The third issue in the Cycle is *land*: both Isaac and Jacob are promised and receive the land of Canaan as part of the divine promise and patriarchal inheritance.

However, it must be emphasized that none of these three factors appears independently. A series of polarities pervade the text and charge it with life force and dramatic tension. The first issue, birth, functions together with its opposite: barrenness. The contrastive pair *barrenness/fertility*, in its variety of expressions, lies at the heart of the personal anxieties of Rebekkah and Rachel, and the interpersonal tensions between Rachel and Leah. The fact that all the major women in Genesis, and many outside it, are initially barren and struggle for their matriarchal inheritance is undoubtedly a hint at the continuity of the curse of Eden. But the various tensions over childbirth also bring to expression deep anxieties over cultural continuity, and a one-dimensional perspective on the role of the female in a patriarchal world. Esau, it will be recalled, is reproached for his breach of endogamy in 26:34ff. (cf. 27:46 and 28:9), and the concern for continuity through a true line also motivates Isaac's blessing in 28:1ff. The tension is also brought to negative expression in the episode of Dinah's rape by the uncircumcised Shechemites in chapter 34.

The second issue, blessing, also functions together with its opposite. The contrastive pair *nonblessing/blessing* underpins the motivations, strife and actions of Rebekkah, Jacob, Isaac, and Esau. Indeed, the desire for blessing is a primary driving power of Genesis 25:19–35:22. Its counterpoint can also be characterized as *curse*, as the very language of the narrative indicates. After Rebekkah urges Jacob to deceive Isaac, Jacob says he fears he might receive a curse *(qelalah)* instead of the blessing (27:12). Similarly, when Isaac blesses Jacob, he says: "those who curse you will be cursed (stem: *'arar*), and those who bless you will be blessed" (27:29; cf. 12:3). It may also be noted that the issue of blessing is of interpersonal importance in Jacob's relations with Laban (30:27,30) and Esau (33:17). The hope for a blessing and fear of a curse clearly charge the actions of this Cycle.

Land functions in this Cycle as subject of the binary pair *exile/homeland*. The actions of Genesis 25:19–35:22 can thus be viewed along a spatial axis. Jacob flees from Canaan and has an encounter with the divine at the border shrine of Beth-el (28:10ff.); he stays in Aram until Rachel gives birth, whereupon he returns and encounters the divine at the border shrines of Mahanayim and Penuel (chapter 32). The shrines mark the transition of action from sacred to profane space, and back. The promises of land inheritance in the divine blessings to Isaac (26:4,24) and Jacob (28:13;35:12) underscore this value of settlement on the land as a sign of divine grace and favor. Only when Jacob resettles in Canaan is his patriarchal destiny confirmed (chap. 35).

The fundamental significance of the issues of birth, blessing, and land in the Jacob Cycle is further corroborated by the fact that they constitute the divine promise given to Abraham (12:1–3). The fact that blessing promises appear at the beginning and end of each of the life cycles of Abraham, Isaac, and Jacob serves to intensify the inner tensions in each cycle involving barrenness and exile. The values and struggles reflected in the Jacob narrative are nuanced repeatedly in the Book of Genesis. They further surface in covenantal texts, particularly in the Book of Deuteronomy, where the promise of covenantal fidelity is also life/fertility, blessing, and homeland. By contrast, covenantal perfidy is threatened with death, barrenness, curse and exile.

It is, finally, most striking that these tensions in the patriarchal cycles, which are continued in the covenantal texts, constitute the inner structure of the Eden narrative (Genesis 3). Eden was a sacred spatial center in which all manner of blessing and life abounded. The primary life values of fertile womb and fertile earth, of life and blessing, were lost through the action of Adam and Eve: earth and womb were cursed, and mankind was exiled from sacred space. As seen in an earlier chapter, these values were retrieved both by Noah (Genesis 9) and by Abraham (12:1-3).

The three binary tensions examined, expressed through the interpersonal dynamics and tensions of the patriarchal narratives, undoubtedly reflect deep hopes and anxieties in ancient Israelite culture. The power of the Jacob Cycle, as with the patriarchal texts generally, is that it provides personal focus for recurrent cultural-national issues: the struggle for blessing and confirmation, the threat of discontinuity and rejection, the conflicts between and within generations, and the wrestling for rebirth, name, and destiny. The final irony, not lost on the narrator, albeit handled with circumspect silence, is that all the interpersonal machinations of the protagonists and antagonists are but the actualization of a predetermined fate, of a forecasted divine determination (cf. the oracles to Jacob and Joseph, in Genesis 27 and 37). Accordingly, no unpromised fire is stolen from heaven. To the contrary—those whom God has chosen succeed. But in the thickness of historical time, and because of limited divine interventions, realization of the divine promises appears to rest with human action. Just this narrative perspective—the ambilateral givenness and hiddenness of divine grace—gives to the Jacob Cycle its most fulsome power.[15]

4. Exodus 1-4/The Prologue to the Exodus Cycle

In the Book of Exodus, the several groups of ancestors which were recorded in the Book of Genesis as the sons of Jacob-Israel (Gen. 35:23-26; 46:8-27) are transformed into a nation: the sons/people of Israel. The process is gradual and deliberate. The genealogy of Jacob and his clan, recorded in Genesis 46:8-27, is repeated in Exodus 1:1-5, so that a link is forged between it and the preceding patriarchal narratives. Indeed, the transitional function of this genealogy can best be appreciated from a structural point of view: the last verse in the Book of Genesis, Genesis 50:26 ("Then Joseph died at 110 years, and they embalmed him so that he was encased in a mummy in Egypt"), is recapitulated in Exodus 1:6 ("Then Joseph died, together with his brethren and that entire generation"), thereby framing the intervening genealogy. With the resumption of the plot line, the "sons of Israel" of v.1 are called "the *nation* of the sons of Israel" in v.9. The stage is thus set for the national epic of liberation which follows.

The Books of Genesis and Exodus are linked not only by this stress on ethnic continuity but by thematic considerations as well. Joseph, on his deathbed, tells his sons that "Elohim will surely *remember* you and bring you up from this land to the land which He foreswore to Abraham, Isaac, and Jacob" (Genesis 50:25). This promise is alluded to at an early point in Exodus: When the Israelites suffered from the travail of their Egyptian bondage, "Elohim *remembered*" His covenantal promise to the patriarchs (2:24). This promise and remembrance are again referred to in the traditions recording Moses' initial encounters with the ancestral God of the patriarchs (cf. Exodus 3:16-17 with Genesis 50:25, and Exodus 6:3-5 with Exodus 2:23-26), so that the divine appearances to Moses are also linked to the chain of promises to the patriarchs in Genesis.

Another more striking link between Genesis and Exodus is provided by the oracle of Genesis 15:13-15, which announces a considerable delay in the fulfillment of the divine promises of the inheritance of Canaan. According to this oracle prophecy, Abraham's seed would first be a dweller *(ger)* in a land not their own (i.e., Egypt), where they would also be enslaved *(va'avadum)* and tormented *(ve'innu)* for 400 years. Thereupon, the oracle concludes, Israel would leave that land—Egypt— and return "here" (i.e., to Canaan). These themes and this language are echoed in the opening chapters of Exodus, as if to alert the reader that the preconditions set by the Genesis oracle are now being realized. Hence, one reads that the Egyptians enslaved *(vaya'avidu,* 1:13) the Israelites, and tormented them *('anoto,* 1:11); that Moses named his son Gershom, for "I have become a dweller *(ger)* in a foreign land" (2:22); and that God promised the Israelites the riches of Egypt (3:22), even as had been foretold in Genesis 15:14.

Considerable literary effort was thus expended to link the patriarchal histories of Genesis with the Egyptian sojourn of Exodus. Moreover, the last example, which foreshadows the termination of Israelite servitude by allusions to the oracle in Genesis, brings us to the main concern of the present chapter. The opening chapters of the Book of Exodus (1-4) will be shown to foreshadow the events and scenarios of chapters 5-19. To fully appreciate this stylization of the ancient record, Exodus 1-19 must be seen for what it is: a literary construct fusing saga and history.

The exodus from Egypt was experienced as an event of divine redemption, during which ancient promises were realized and divine power confirmed. The transformative nature of this event in the lives of the ancient Israelites affected its recollection and literary formulation. For those who experienced it, no simple chronological report would do justice to the wonder of the divine intervention in their historical lives. Only the saga form would do, focusing selectively on specific events and people, endowing the encounters between the principal actors with a paradigmatic cast, and infusing historical process with the wonder of supernatural events.[1]

Seen in this light, Exodus 1-19 is a presentation of the "events" of the Egyptian bondage and liberation through the prism of religious memory and imagination. The biblical focus is, accordingly, on divine power and will, on human hope and intransigence, on Moses and the Israelites, on Pharaoh and the Egyptians. Factual details become secondary to a dramatization of the inner conviction that with the exodus-event the God of the patriarchs has fulfilled His ancient promises. The narrative style is cast in a rhythm of alternating plagues and dialogues, so that the pace of events has a liturgical, climactic effect. The mystery and forms of divine providence are ever present, foreshadowing events to come.

The opening depiction of the Israelites in Exodus 1 sets the tone: "And the Israelites were fruitful and plentiful; they multiplied and became very powerful until the land was filled with them" (v.7). This situation—which has the overtones of a new creation and beginning—is reemphasized by Pharaoh's corresponding assertion: "Behold, the Israelites have become more numerous and powerful than we" (v.9). To keep his control over them he institutes two measures of population control, both of which backfire. First the Israelites are forced to build store-cities. "But the more they were oppressed the more they increased and spread" (v.12). The second measure is even more drastic: infanticide. According to Pharaoh's decree, all firstborn male Israelites are to be killed. However, because of the resourcefulness and piety of the midwives (v.17), the Israelites were able to avert this danger and so increase in number that the Pharaoh was impelled to reissue and stiffen his earlier decree: "Every newborn male must be thrown into the Nile, although every female may be kept alive" (v.22).

All these events set the backdrop for the hero Moses. Hidden in an ark, and thereby saved from the calamitous decree, Moses is drawn forth alive from the waters of the Nile (2:1–10).

With the rescue of Moses, the scene shifts abruptly. Once singled out, the hero immediately assumes his historical destiny. Time is telescoped, actions are highly stylized, and Moses is portrayed from the start as linking his personal fate to that of his people. Thus "Moses grew up, went out to meet his brethren, and saw their toil" (2:11). Shortly thereafter, he intervenes in a fight to save a fellow Israelite and kills the offending Egyptian. When tauntingly called a "prince and judge" of his people, Moses flees to the desert, thereby counterpointing with his freedom the servitude of the Israelites who yet remain in Egypt:

> The Israelites groaned on account of their labor and called out; and their cry for help from their labor went up to Elohim. Elohim heard their tormented plea, and Elohim remembered his covenant with Abraham, Isaac, and Jacob. And so Elohim looked upon the Israelites, and Elohim took heed. (vv.23–25)

With this, the opening chapters conclude: the historical servitude has been described, the hero has been introduced and involved, and God Himself—up until now silent—"took heed."

At this point the narrative, which remains with Moses in the Midianite steppeland, takes a decisive turn. While shepherding his flock, and undoubtedly mindful of the oppression of his brethren enslaved in Egypt, Moses sees a messenger of YHWH near a mountain, at a *sneh*-bush, seemingly enveloped—but unconsumed—by fire. Moses, his daily rhythm disrupted, is addressed: "Remove your sandals from your feet because you are standing on holy ground" (3:5). The event is a theophany of the God of Abraham, Isaac, and Jacob. The promised redemption is now at hand.

The mountain remains a mountain, and the bush a bush. But now all is changed: God has spoken to Moses. The words do not arise from within Moses. To the contrary; he is confronted and commanded by them. "He said: 'Moses, Moses,' and he said: 'Here I am [*hinneni*].'" This address and response hark back to God's earlier speech to Abraham before his final trial (22:1). At the moment of divine address, Moses, like Abraham before him, can only respond with his total presence and submit to its claim over his life. To be sure, he has been preparing for this moment his whole mature life. Indeed, before fleeing Egypt, he had even "acted out" on the body of a taskmaster the liberation and justice that the times required. Now, when God appears to him to fulfill the promise to the patriarchs (vv.6–8), Moses knows that he can never again return to his prior everyday activities. God's revelatory presence has driven a wedge into his lifetime and that of his brethren. His own personal past—where private passion for justice had only produced a random act of resentment—is over.

The divine revelation and new promise thus mark a transformation in Moses' religious consciousness. He is to be a messenger of God to his people (v. 10). But, overcome with insignificance and fear, he balks: "Who am I that I should go to Pharaoh and that I should deliver the Israelites from Egypt?" (v.11). Moses knows what has to be done for God's sake, and for his own integrity. But he fears the cost. He has to surrender his "I," his sense of self, to God's will and command. Sensing this, God responds to Moses' repeated "I's" of v. 11 with: "*I* shall be [*'ehyeh*] with you" (v.12). And to further strengthen his will, He gives Moses a sign "that *I* have sent you" (v.12). This sign is the promise that He would bring him back to this spot after the exodus event.

But as such a sign was for the future, Moses then asks this God to reveal His name—so that the people to whom he will go will be convinced in the immediate present (v.13). The sequence and meaning of the ensuing passage (vv.14-15) is, in the preserved tradition, somewhat garbled; and so scholars have naturally offered many interpretations. Be this as it may, the following point may be underscored. Before the name YHWH is revealed in v.15 to Moses as the name of the ancient God of the patriarchs, a midrashic play on this name is given (v.14)—a "play" of profound theological seriousness, since it serves to characterize this God through His name. God says to Moses that He is *'ehyeh 'asher 'ehyeh*, "I shall be that which I shall be," and that he (Moses) should tell the people, "*'ehyeh* (I shall be) has sent me to you" (v.14). No more, we seem to be cautioned, may be ascribed to God than that. He is the Unconditioned One who shall be as He shall be.

But the Israelites have first to undergo a spiritual transformation in order to trust the words of Moses on behalf of YHWH. Sensing this difficulty—and probably to assure himself as well—Moses requests and receives three new signs from God: his staff could be transformed into a snake, his hand could become leprous, and the Nile waters could be turned to blood (4:1-9). When Moses later shows these signs to the Israelites, the nation "trusted" *(va-ya'amen)* that God had come to redeem His people from their suffering (4:31).

But even after God provides him with supplementary signs to convince the Israelites of his mission, Moses continues to express ambivalence about his task (4:10ff.). He does not question the task itself or its necessity, but he does question his own worthiness. God knows that this apparent humility and lack of self-confidence are a disguised lack of trust in divine providence, and He becomes furious. But Moses' renewed protestation of inability (4:10-16) supplements the earlier one (3:11) and further underscores the "prophetic" dimension of Moses' commission:

> Then Moses said to YHWH; "O my lord, surely I am not a man of words, nor was I yesterday or the day before that, even from the time when You spoke to your servant; but I am heavy of speech and heavy of tongue." But YHWH said to him: "Who gives a man speech, or makes him dumb, or deaf, or sighted, or blind? Is it not me, YHWH? Therefore, go now and I will be with your mouth, and instruct you what to speak." And he said: "Oh my Lord, send

someone else." Then YHWH became enraged at Moses, and said: "What about your brother, Aaron the Levite? He speaks easily and is coming to you, and will be glad to see you. So speak to him and I will put the words in his mouth: I will be with your mouth and with his mouth, and will instruct you both what to do. He shall speak for you to the people. He will be as your mouth, and you will be to him as a god."

In this passage, Moses is presented as a prophet, who, like the ideal stated in Deuteronomy 18:18, has divine words put into his mouth. A prophet is but a vessel, a "formulator" of the divine will that surges to earthly realization through him. Does not God say to Jeremiah that He would be with him and put His words into his mouth (Jeremiah 1:9)? And does He not also say to Jeremiah that "you will be like my mouth" (15:19)? But Moses resists the divine charge, so that, in the end, God says that Aaron will serve him (Moses) as a prophetic mouthpiece.

The two commission and resistance scenes of chapters 3 and 4 would seem to be alternate but complementary literary expressions of one transformative period in Moses' life. Taken together, the following structure of Moses' commission emerges:

1. God speaks (3:4-8)
2. Commission and sending (3:9-10)
3. The prophet resists, claiming to be unworthy and incompetent to be the messenger (3:11; 4:10)
4. God says that He will be with him and his speech (3:12; 4:11-12)
5. The prophet wants signs, or assurances, to bolster his spirit and / or convince those he is charged to address (3:12; 4:1-9).

Comparison of the literary formulation of Moses' commission with that of other prophets reveals instructive parallels:[2]

Exodus 3-4	*Isaiah*	*Jeremiah*	*Ezekiel*
1. Encounter with God	6:1-4	1:5	2:1-2
2. Commission	6:8-10	1:5	2:3-7
3. Resistance / impediment to speech	6:5 1:6		
4. Divine assurance and	6:7	1:7-10, 17-19	1:8-3:3; 3:8-9
Preparation of the speaking mouth of the prophet	6:13	1:9-5	2:8-3:3

In each of the above, a commanding divine presence is felt, and the prophet recoils in fear and expresses inability to speak the word of God. In the case of Isaiah, a divine being purifies his "impure" mouth; in the case of Jeremiah, God says: "I will be with your mouth"; and, in the case of Ezekiel, there is the image of God placing His words into the mouth of the prophet in the form of a scroll. Physical imagery is thus used to communicate the prophet's role as spokesman of God. Similarly, when Moses claims to be "heavy of tongue and heavy of mouth," the issue seems less that of physical deformity than inability and inferiority before God. In the repetition of Moses' commission in Exodus 6, Moses further protests that he is of "uncircumcised lips" (vv.12,30); i.e., that he feels, unable and impure—like Isaiah—to speak God's words.

What emerges from, and is expressed by, the foregoing literary pattern is the prophets' fear of chosenness by God; their terror of being confronted and elected for a task for which they feel unprepared and unworthy; and their realization that it is only by the grace of God's active presence that they are enabled to perform the task. This kind of dynamic bears a striking phenomenological resemblance to testimonies by artists who feel themselves in the grip of an overwhelming force at the moment of inspiration, mere vessels for bringing that "will" to formal realization.[3]

On his way back to Egypt, after receiving the three additional signs enumerated in 4:1-9, and after the just-discussed recommission scene of 4:10-16, Moses is again addressed by God (4:21b-23):

> Note all these signs [*mofetim*] which I have given you and perform them before Pharaoh. But I shall harden his heart and he will not release the people. Then you will say to Pharaoh: "Thus says YHWH: Israel is my firstborn; therefore I say to you, release my son that he may worship me. And if you refuse to release him, I shall surely kill your own firstborn."

A new matter is introduced here. For the signs "which I have given you" are now expressly intended for the Pharaoh as well, not just the Israelites. Indeed, God says that if Pharaoh will not respond to the signs and release the Israelites He, YHWH, will kill Pharaoh's own firstborn son.

A similar double motivation for the "signs" appears in the extended plague-cycle of chapters 7-12:36. Thus, whereas it is stated in 7:3-5 that the signs to come are for the Egyptians who will, thereby, "come to know" the power of YHWH, 10:1-2 states that they are *also* intended for the Israelites: "in order that you will tell your sons and daughters what I did in Egypt...and know that I am YHWH."

One may go further. Not only does Exodus 4:21*b*-23 serve to anticipate the plagues forecast against the Egyptians in general terms, it also has a *specific*, structural relation to them. It may thus be noted that Exodus 4:21*b*-23, by virtue of its allusion to 4:1-9, includes three signs *plus* a climactic fourth (the killing of the firstborn) to be enacted before Pharaoh. This pattern of one triad plus a climax (3+1) formally anticipates the overall plague cycle (7:8-12:36) which is composed of three triads plus a climax in which firstborn males are killed (3+3+3+1).[4] The fact that two shorter versions of this pattern (two triads with climactic fourth parts in which firstborn are killed) can also be found in the historical liturgies of Psalms 78 (vv.43-51) and 105 (vv.27-36) further strengthens the likelihood that Exodus 4:21*b*-23 is itself a variation on this structural form. While the climactic event in 4:21*b*-23 is not explicitly called a sign, there can be little doubt as to its intent and functions.

However, while there is a literary symmetry in the pattern of the plagues forecast against the Egyptians (3+1 and 3+3+3+1), an asymmetry apparently remains. The plagues in Exodus 7:8-12:36 are, as noted, meant for the Egyptians *and* the Israelites (cf. 7:3-5 and 10:1-2), whereas the triad-plus-climax structure of signs in 4:21*b*-23 does not explicitly refer to the Israelites. There does not, then, seem to be a fourth sign for them. If the death of the Egyptian firstborn in Exodus 12 is balanced by the life and liberation of the Israelites, no counterpoint seems to occur to offset the death of Pharaoh's firstborn son mentioned in 4:23. Instead, a most unsettling event is described (vv.24-26):

> And on the way, at a resting spot, YHWH encountered him and sought to kill him. Then Zipporah took a flint and cut off the foreskin of her son, and touched his penis, saying: "You are now a bridegroom of blood with YHWH."* So he released him, and she said: "You are a bridegroom of blood through the circumcision."

This text is heavy with mystery and has confused generations of interpreters—for the context and various pronominal

---

*I accept S. Talmon's view that *LY*, in "bridegroom of blood *LY*" is an abbreviation for *Le-YHWH*, "with YHWH." It stands parallel to the succeeding ritual expression *La-molat*, "through the circumcision."[5]

references are indeterminate. All that seems clear, at the most basic level, is that Moses was attacked by God on his return to Egypt. On the basis of the literary-structural remarks just offered, however, a symbolical understanding may now be offered. Just as 4:23 anticipates the death of the Egyptians through the figure of Pharaoh's firstborn, so do vv.24-26 anticipate the redemption of the Israelites, God's own firstborn (cf. v.23), by focusing on the salvation and protection effected for Moses by the blood of his own son's circumcision. Moses and his firstborn thus counterpoint Pharaoh and his firstborn. Since this episode regarding Moses and his son *immediately follows* vv.21-23 and its pattern of triad-plus-climax, a corresponding 3+1 structure of signs also seems to obtain for the Israelites (i.e. 4:1-9, 24-26).

These literary-structural considerations may be complemented by a focus on 4:24-26 from the viewpoint of Moses' spiritual biography—for his life was not simply symbolic of national destiny, but was private and individual on its own terms. The narrative of Moses in Midian, 3:1-4:23, makes it clear that he is beset by doubts and ambivalences as regards his prophetic task. Perhaps due to the confusing and disrupting events of his childhood, Moses finds it initially difficult to trust a god who says He would "be as He would be." Now, at this most decisive moment in his life, when he gathers his strength to submit himself fully to God as a faithful messenger, Moses is tested in his resolve, in his capacity to acknowledge that He who referred to Himself as *'eheyeh*, "I shall be," is the same One whether He promises life and redemption or causes death and destruction. A true messenger, one faithful to his task, would have to know this truth and not resist it.[6]

At all events, the narrator has undoubtedly transformed an ancient, even demonic, literary fragment in order to provide a dramatic externalization of an interior moment in Moses' spiritual life. Moses, who feels himself attacked by this life-promising God, is helped through his crises by his wife Zipporah, who turns his attention to his son and the future generation which his mission will ultimately benefit. Following this event Moses arrives in Egypt and displays the three signs given him to the Israelite elders (4:27–30), who immediately "trust" God's promise (4:31). The signs to Pharaoh and the Egyptians have yet to be given.

Before considering how Exodus 1-4 foreshadows Exodus 5-19, a brief clarification is due concerning the decision to limit the opening textual unit to the end of chapter 4. That this delimitation is not at all self-evident is easily confirmed by the fact that the breakdown of the various narrative subunits from Exodus 4:18 on are not clearly marked. The particular relationship of Exodus 5 to its textual environment is representative of the difficulties involved, and of direct pertinence to our present concern: Is Exodus 5 to be included with 4:18–6:1, as part of the return to Egypt (even though the signs of chapter 4 are nowhere mentioned when Moses and Aaron go before Pharaoh), or does it begin a new narrative sequence?[7]

To answer this question several considerations are determinative, to my mind. First, the scene shifts back to Egypt only in Exodus 5, to which the preceding chapter is both a transition and an anticipation of tasks to be done. Second, there are many verbal and thematic echos between Exodus 5 and the mise-en-scène of the Israelite servitude in Egypt in Exodus 1 (see discussion below), thus suggesting a renewed—though altogether new—stage in the drama of oppression and redemption. And third, it is precisely the failure of Moses before Pharaoh (chap. 5), together with Moses' sense of the countervailing effect of the revealed name (v.23), which provide the motivation and apologia for the recommission scene in 6:22ff. Accordingly, the common tendency to separate Exodus 5 from what follows would appear to snap a deliberate narrative web (particularly compare 5:23 with 6:2–3).

Thus both because of its distinctions from chapter 4, and its links with chapter 6, Exodus 5 would seem to begin a new narrative phase. In it Moses and Aaron appear before Pharaoh in Egypt with the divine name and demand. To be sure, such an analytic estimation, based as it is on literary-typological considerations, is a meta-analysis arising from the *received* narrative tradition. For from the viewpoint of the distinguishable sources or traditions which comprise the narrative, Exodus 6:2ff. is linguistically distinct from—and even thematically contradictory to—chapter 5. But one may not doubt that these and many other compositional problems facing the reader of the Exodus Cycle are conditioned by a double concern of the final arranger-composer: to both preserve diverse traditions (e.g., the two commission traditions noted earlier) *and* to transform them into one continuous narrative. It is, in fact, the suggestion of the following analysis that it was precisely in the process of weaving together a continuous narrative from multiple oral and literary traditions that the final arranger-composer stylized his materials typologically, so that the opening narrative (in Exodus 1-4) linguistically and thematically foreshadows or balances that which follows (in Exodus 5-19).

Some of the links between the opening chapters of the Book of Exodus and their sequel have already been intimated. Here, now, follows a fuller explication of interrelations which obtain between the opening unit of the Book of Exodus (Part I, chapters 1-4) and its successor (Part II, chapters 5-19).

1. In Exodus 1:8-14 (Part I), the toil of the Israelites is levied by Pharaoh because they have become numerous (*rav*, v.7). When Moses and Aaron later go to the Pharaoh to request the release of the Israelites (5:5-19, Part II), he increases their toil because they have become even more numerous (*rabbim*, v.5). That Pharaoh is a new one, who has ascended during Moses' absence in the Midianite wilderness (2:23). The new unit (chap. 5) thus begins with a decree imposed by the (new) Pharaoh, even as did the first (1:8-11).

2. In Part I, a second method is employed to curb the growth of the Israelites: infanticide of male firstborn. Their babies are to be drowned in the sea (Exodus 1:22); but Moses is saved (2:1-6). In Part II, the Egyptians are drowned in the sea, while all Israel is saved (chaps. 14-15).

3. The first commission of Moses (Part I) occurs at the *sneh*-bush (2:3), adjacent to a "mountain of God" (v.1). Later (Part II), after the Exodus, all Israel stands at *Sinai*, a "mountain of God" (Exodus 24:13). The link is structural and linguistic.

4. In 3:6-11 and 4:10-17 (Part I) Moses is commissioned and complains of his inability to speak—of being "heavy of tongue." His brother Aaron is thereupon designated his spokesman. As part of the commission, God reveals Himself as God of the fathers (3:6, 16), refers to the covenant-promise (3:7-9, 17-20), and states that the God of the fathers is known as EHYeH (v.14). These several features are replicated in Part II: during the course of the succeeding events, God reveals Himself to Moses as El Shaddai, God of the fathers (6:2), refers to the covenant-promise (vv.4-8), and reveals His name: YHWH. Moses, in turn, complains that he is of "uncircumcised lips" (6:12, 30). As with the previous phrase "heavy of tongue," this phrase equally refers to Moses' own sense of incompetence; and, as in Part I (4:14-17), Aaron is again designated Moses' substitute (7:1-2). This second tradition of the commission serves to recommit Moses to his task and, as Greenberg has

plausibly suggested, to stress the divine name YHWH and to introduce the central theme-idea of the second part: that Egyptians and Israelites alike must come to see that He is God.[8]

5. In Part I, God gives Moses three signs, plus a fourth (4:1–9, 24–26), so that the Israelites will trust him (4:5, 8,9). The first three signs are intended also for the Egyptians, while the killing of the firstborn is a sign directed to Pharaoh alone (4:21–23). These traditions appear in Part II in expanded form. They reappear as 10 plagues, or signs, taking the form 3+3+3+1. Strikingly, this triple literary triad was already detected in early Rabbinic times, as is evidenced by Rabbi Judah bar Ilai's Hebrew acronym for the plagues, memorialized in the Passover Haggadda: *DeTZaKH,'ADaSH, Be'AHaV.*[9]

6. The fourth sign of the first sequence (Exodus 4), and the tenth sign of the second (chapters 11–12), each involve the killing of firstborn Egyptians, in contrast to the redemption of Israelites, the firstborn of God. The protecting power of blood benefits the Israelites in each case. In Part II, the Israelites are protected by blood during the night of the paschal feast—when all the firstborn Egyptian males were killed (12:7–13). In Exodus 4:24–26 (Part I), Moses is protected by the circumcision blood of his firstborn. Early recognition of the thematic connection between Exodus 4:24–26, dealing with the apotropeic, or protective power of the blood of circumcision, and Exodus 12:13 where a similar power of blood recurs, can be found in the ancient Palestinian Targum traditions and the medieval Bible commentary by Rabbi Abraham ibn Ezra.

7. When Moses first showed the signs to the Israelites (4:27ff.), the nation "trusted" (*vayya'amen*, v.31), even as all the Israelites later "trusted" (*vayya'aminu, 14:31*) in God and His servant Moses after the final manifestation of power against the Egyptians.

8. And finally, the encounter between Moses and God in 3:1ff. occurs at the mountain of God-Elohim, by a *sneh*-bush. The original confirmation sign by God to Moses at the commission was that after the exodus the people would "worship Elohim at this mountain" (v.12). The geographical reference "at this mountain" is, according to many scholars, the *sneh*-bush referred to in vv.1–4. And indeed, after the exodus the people do go to a mountain called "mountain of Elohim" (24:13), also called *Sinai* (19:11,20), located in the wilderness of Sin (19:1–2). The thematic link between the units

is thus further underscored by the acoustical similarity of *sneh*/Sinai.

The function of the foreshadowing in Part I is to interconnect the saga-cycle by means of recurrent images and language. While these interrelations are inobtrusively textured into the overall cycle, their analysis enhances our appreciation of the narrative art of Exodus 1–19 and reveals the inner-textual issues which occupied its author's imagination. The various dimensions of the foreshadowing cycle can be recapitulated and further expanded through the following detailed chart.

Exodus 1–4	*Exodus 5–19*
1. The Egyptians embitter the Israelites' labor (*sivlotam*) through mortar and *(livenim)* bricks; 1:11–14.	After Moses and Aaron appear before Pharaoh their labor (*sivlotam*) is made difficult through straw and bricks (*livenim*); 5:4ff.
2. For they have multiplied *(vayirbu)*; 1:7, cf. 9:12.	For, Pharaoh says, "Indeed, the people are many" (*rabbim*); 5:5.
3. Pharaoh commands that every Israelite male be thrown into the Nile; 1:22.	At the Exodus, "God threw the chariots of Pharaoh and his retinue into the sea"; 14:15–15:19.
4. But Moses is saved; 2:1ff.	But the Israelites are saved; 14:15–15:19.
5. YHWH appears to Moses at the *sneh*, the mountain of God; 3:1-2.	YHWH appears to Moses (6:2ff.), and all Israelites at *Sinai*, the mountain of God; 19:1ff.
6. The God of the fathers hears the cry of His people and prepares to bring them to Canaan, the Promised Land 3:6-8.	The God of the fathers hears the wail of His people and remembers His promise to bring them to Canaan; 6:4-8.
7. At his commission, Moses is fearful (3:11) and complains that he is "heavy of mouth and tongue," 4:10, so God says: "Aaron will be to you as a mouth, and you will be to him as an Elohim," 4:14–16.	At his commission, Moses is fearful and complains that he is of "uncircumcised lips," 6:12, 30, so God says: "See I have appointed you Elohim to Pharaoh, and your brother, Aaron, will be your prophet," 7:1.

8. YHWH instructs the Israelites, through Moses, to take (stem: *sha'al*) silver, etc. from the Egyptians and to despoil (stem: *natzal*) them at the Exodus: 3:21–22.

"And the Israelites did according to Moses' instructions" and took all (stem: *sha'al*) silver utensils from Egypt, so that they despoiled (stem: *natzal*) the Egyptians; 12:35–36.

9. 3 + 1 signs are given for the Israelites (and also the Egyptians); 4:2ff.

9 + 1 signs occur for the Egyptians (and also the Israelites); 7–11.

10. The fourth sign to Pharoah involves the death of his firstborn; 4:23.

The tenth sign to Pharoah involves the death of Egyptian firstborn; 11:1ff.

11. The apotropeic power of blood deflects divine wrath; 4:24ff.

The apotropeic power of blood deflects divine destruction; 12:7ff.

12. The signs are displayed before the nation…and it believed *(vayya'amen)*; 4:31.

At the sea "all Israel saw the the mighty hand and believed *(vayya'minu)* in YHWH"; 14:31.

We began this chapter by indicating several anticipatory links between the Book of Genesis and the Book of Exodus. It may be appropriate to close with another. The exodus event so dominated Israelite theological and historiographical imagination that it affected even the formulation of the Abrahamic traditions. A hint in this direction occurs at the very beginning of the Patriarchal Cycle, in Genesis 12:10–20. Immediately after his entrance into the land, Abram *migrates* to *Egypt* because of famine *(ra'av)* and sojourns (stem: *gwr*) there. After an episode in which he introduced his wife, Sarah, as his sister—thereby setting the stage for Pharaoh's amorous advances—YHWH brings plagues (stem: *naga'*) against Pharaoh and his household (v.17). In response, the Pharaoh sends (stem: *shalah*) him out of Egypt, where he has accumulated great wealth (v.16; 13:1). Both the narrative and language of Genesis 12:10–20 are clearly reminiscent of the Exodus Cycle, where *shalah* and *gwr* are common terms, and *naga'* is used regarding a plague in 11:1. This profound effect of the exodus on biblical imagination will be the subject of a later discussion (see chap. 10).

Speeches and Prayers

5. Deuteronomy 6:20-25 / Teaching and Transmission

As we have seen, one of the divine motivations recorded for the wonders in Egypt was that the power of God be retold to future generations.

> Then YHWH said to Moses: "Go in before Pharaoh's presence; for I have hardened his and his courtiers' hearts—in order that I may place these my signs in his midst, and in order that you may tell your sons and grandchildren all my deeds in Egypt, and my signs which I have put among them, that you all know that I am YHWH." (Exodus 10:1-2)

This motivation to "tell the tale" for the benefit of future generations undoubtedly energized the narrator of the Exodus Cycle. Psalm 78 also begins with similar motivation for the preservation and recitation of the patriarchal and exodus traditions, and further voices the belief that knowledge of them would support trust in YHWH and observance of His Torah (vv.1-8). This need to transmit sacred memories was early acknowledged as necessary for cultural and religious continuity. It is just this issue that underlies the sermon in Deuteronomy 6:20-25, which follows:

> If your son asks you tomorrow saying: "What is the purpose of the testimonies, and laws and judgments which YHWH our God has commanded you?" Then you shall say to your son: "We were slaves of Pharoah in Egypt, and YHWH our God took us from Egypt with a mighty arm. And YHWH placed fearsome and bad signs and wonders in Egypt, before our eyes, against Pharaoh and his household. And He took us from there to bring us [here] and to give us the land which He promised our forefathers. And YHWH commanded us to observe all these laws, to fear YHWH our God, that it may be good for us always and sustain us as [they have done so even] to this day. And we shall be successful* if we observe and do all this commandment before our God as He has commanded us."

---

*The precise meaning of *tzedaqah* here is difficult. Targum Ongelos translated it *zekuta*, "merit"; Buber-Rosenzweig translated it *Bewährung*, "preservation."

79

For Deuteronomy 6:20-25, the exodus event and the covenantal laws are the central religious realities which transformed the sons of Israel-Jacob into the people of Israel. This sermon has been credited to Moses, and is included among several reflective and hortatory speeches in Deuteronomy 1-11. Speaking shortly before he died, but unable to share in the conquest of the land, Moses wants to make sure that the traditions and laws of his and earlier generations will be transmitted by those entering Canaan to their sons. He thus anticipates the future and the responsibility to guide succeeding generations towards participation in the legacy of the communal past. Most essentially, this text signals the importance of education in any attempt to transform the memories and obligations of the fathers into the living actuality of the sons. Being a speech which projects an instruction scene for those who will inherit the land, the text is deeply set within the temporal dialectic of present-future.[1] As Moses instructs his people, and is concerned with the continuity of memory and creed, so should you—the text appears to say—who hear these words take his model and concern seriously.

The sermon begins with a hypothetical condition ("If your son") and continues with an assertive resolution ("Then you shall"). The conditional clause includes a question from son to father which discloses the former's lack of knowledge and commitment to the covenant traditions of his father. The son distances himself from his father by referring to the law as that "which YHWH...has commanded *you*." In the Greek translation of the Torah (the Septuagint), and in citations found in Oriental versions of the Passover Haggadah, the reading is *'otanu* ("us"), and not *'etkhem* ("you," pl.). The reading in our Massoretic text, however, seems less a scribal error as much as a variant formulation designed to bring to consciousness just that psychosocial dynamic which underlies the son's question. The son's use of the pronoun "you" suggests that he considers himself alien to and uninvolved with the covenant commitments of his father.

By contrast, the historical assertion by the father discloses both knowledge of and commitment to the covenant of Israel. Whereas the son's question distantiates him from his father and fellow-convenanters ("you"), the father's answer seeks to incorporate his son in his answer. His use of the pronoun "us" bridges the gap of culture and experience which the son, who was born in the land and never anticipated it as promise or hope, had expressed. The father thus assumes an unbroken continuity from the days of the exodus to the present. It is probably for this reason that he answers his son's question after a historical prologue.

The son asks: "What [is the purpose of] the testimonies... which YHWH...has commanded you?" The interrogative clause is elliptical here, and must be supplemented. The context gives no reason to assume that the questioner requests information about the *contents* of the covenantal teaching. Indeed, the father's answer proceeds to state the underlying *purposes* of the law: that it is a "good," "sustaining" force for the "benefit" of the covenantal community. Not one word regarding the content of the testimonies is uttered. Even the historical prologue serves less to provide content than to serve the purpose of outlining the gracious acts of God for Israel which, reciprocally, obligate them to Him. This prologue refers to the exodus and the conquest, whereby the promises to the patriarchs were fulfilled. The son who was born in the land, and has perhaps thought that all was due to his powers and prowess, is now informed that he is but the beneficiary of an earlier promise (cf. Deuteronomy 7:1-8), and consequently has a historical debt and obligation.

Deuteronomy 6:20-25 discloses a tension between two generations' memories, sets of experiences, and commitments. It questions the ability of fathers to transmit their laws and faith to their sons, who see these as alien and do not feel the same responsibility concerning them. But, one wonders, is there any reason to expect these sons to be obligated through the memories and achievements of their fathers? That the fathers would want a continuity through their sons of their special relationship with God is understandable. But what was subjective and immediate to them is seen as objective and mediate to their sons. These latter have not experienced the experiences of the fathers, nor have they subjectivized and internalized them. One, in fact, suspects that Moses felt this intergenerational tension most poignantly. He undoubtedly felt, so shortly before his death, full dependence on generational continuity for the realization of his labors.

The teaching of the fathers in Deuteronomy 6:20-25 is an attempt to involve their sons in the covenant community of the future, and undoubtedly reflects the sociological reality of the settlement in Canaan. The attempt by fathers to transform their uninvolved sons from *"dis*temporaries" to *con*temporaries, i.e., time-life sharers, is an issue of supreme and recurrent significance in the Bible.[2] We shall explore it at some length in our discussion of the exodus motif in a later chapter. But two cases may serve to exemplify our point here.

It has long been noted that Exodus 15, the victory hymn recited by Moses after the crossing of the Reed Sea, is divided into two parts. The first part (vv.1-11) deals with the final phase of the redemption from Egypt, namely the deliverance from the sea; whereas the second part (vv.12-18) deals with the period of the conquest of Canaan and with the temple-shrine of the Lord. Although scholars have long debated the historical origin of this hymn, and its motivating impulses, what concerns us here is the striking conjunction, indeed, the fusion, of the reality of the exodus with that of the conquest.[3] For the composer-redactor the miraculous event of crossing the Jordan and conquering the land was a repetition of the wonder of the Reed Sea generations before. But for such a fusion to gain currency, it must have reflected not just an abstract sense of historical parallelism but a deep inner reality of religious consciousness. The "sons" of the conquest generation undoubtedly felt that they experienced redemptive events like those of their "fathers." They concretized this religio-historical understanding by fusing these two separate events of divine redemption into one song of praise.

A similar literary collocation of the exodus and the conquest, arising from their prior fusion in the religious imagination, is to be found in Psalm 114. Here, as in Exodus 15, the "sons" express the felt unity of their contemporary experience of divine power (the conquest) with events of the historical past; specifically, the salvific events surrounding the exodus from Egypt. Their liturgy testifies that for them, too, the crossing of the Jordan River was a miracle of redemption continuous with, if not equivalent to, that of the crossing of the Reed Sea (vv.3,5):

> The sea looked and fled;
>> The Jordan turned tail in fright.
> Why do you flee, O sea;
>> O Jordan, why do you turn tail?

These couplets, paralleling the Reed Sea and the Jordan River are set against the historical background "when Israel departed from Egypt."[4]

Despite their temporal and experiential differences of the two preceding liturgical hymns, one hears in Exodus 15 and Psalm 114 of "sons" who see themselves as the spiritual contemporaries of their "fathers." They perceived their history and experience as shared, and chose common images to give it expression. But just this is *not* the case in Deuteronomy 6:20. By their question the sons show themselves to stand outside the experiences of their fathers, who, on the other hand, presumptively try to involve them in their own memories and obligations, and say: "*we* were"; took *us* out"; "before *our* eyes"; "brought *us*"; "good for *us*"; "commanded *us*."

The fathers are bidden by Moses to reveal their understanding of time and history to their sons. These latter must respond and answer for the sake of religious continuity. When God first spoke to Abram, and he responded, a new religious destiny entered history. His sons all accepted the commitment of their ancestor to a God who had first sent him into a new land with promises. Moses, himself a father of his people, continues this commitment during the dark days of the Egyptian bondage, and is enjoined to help bring the promises of the "god of the fathers" to fruition (Exodus 3:6–9; 6:2–8). Moses' commission is thus also an axial point along the way, as is the covenantal dedication of the entire people at Sinai. From that latter event on, continuity would depend not simply on divine grace and familial obligation but on an ongoing communal commitment to the covenant. As Moses teaches the covenant to the people, so each father is to teach its obligations to his own sons. In Deuteronomy 6:20–25, Moses forewarns future generations that everything would depend on the continuity of spiritual history. The response of the sons is not preserved.

6. Psalm 19 / Creation, Torah, and Hope

The preceding discussion focused on Deuteronomy 6:20-25 and its emphasis on the bounty of covenantal observance. As is clear from various other sermons in Deuteronomy 5-11, that bounty is particularly one of physical sustenance on the land promised to the patriarchs. By contrast, Psalm 19, whose discussion follows, focuses on the spiritual sustenance of the Covenant teaching and places it within a cosmic context of divine beneficence. While the speaker of the psalm has neither an abrogated nor antagonistic relationship to the commandments of God, his relationship to them is nevertheless complicated. The psalmist appeals to God for personal redemption from his present spiritual travail. The text of his prayer follows.

For the Choirmaster
A Psalm of David
The heavens recount the Splendor of El;
the firmament bespeaks His handiwork.
Day transmits speech to day;
Night speaks knowledge to night.
And this without speech or words—
For their voice is not heard.
Their sound covers the earth;
Their words reach the rim of space.
He has given the sun a tent therein.
And it is like a bridegroom leaving his bower,
Going its way like a rejoicing hero.
It rises at the rim of heaven,
And turns its arc at its outreach.
Nothing is hidden from its shrine.

The Torah of YHWH is pure,
Restoring the soul.
The Covenant of YHWH is trustworthy,
Instructing the simple.
The Precepts of YHWH are just,
Rejoicing the heart.
The Command of YHWH is clear,
Enlightening the eyes.
The Splendor of YHWH is pure,

Enduring forever.
> The Laws of YHWH are just,
> Being righteous altogether.
They are worth more than all fine gold;
They are sweeter than honey that drips from the comb.

Even Your servant is made resplendent by them;
There is much gain in their observance.
> But who can know unwitting faults?
> O clear me from hidden errors.
Even restrain Your servant from willful errors;
May they not coerce me.
> Then I will become pure,
> And be cleared from all iniquity.
May the words of my mouth and the thoughts
of my mind find favor before You, YHWH,
my rock and my redeemer.

The concerns and references of this psalm raise this question about it: Is it a hymn, a didactic praise of Torah, or a petition? An attentive reading of its totality suggests that it is, in fact, all three. Its first subsection (vv.2-7) is a *hymn*, with the creation—especially the sun—as its subject; the second part (vv.8-11) is *praise* for the divine teaching, the Torah; and the third part (vv.12-15) is a *petition* for divine aid against sins of omission and commission. But while each of the parts presents a distinct subject in a distinct style, the psalm is a unity. Indeed, it is precisely in the interface between the generic diversity of its subsections and its received unity that the religious meaning of Psalm 19 lies and unfolds.

Preliminary access to the meaning and internal cohesion of this psalm comes by way of the ancient Near East. N. Sarna, elaborating upon an insight of modern commentators on Psalm 19, has emphasized a striking feature of parts 1 and 2 when seen against the context of the Near Eastern world of hymnody. He notes that both part 1, whose specific subject is the sun, and part 2, whose subject is the Torah, are dominated by epithets and phraseology commonly found in ancient Egyptian, Hittite, and Mesopotamian hymns to the sun.[1] Accordingly, Sarna has suggested that there could well be a polemical basis to this psalm; namely, that a pagan hymn to the sun has been displaced and superseded by a hymn to Torah which uses the same imagery.[2] Hymns to the virtues of Torah are not unknown in the psalter and appear in Psalms 1 and 119, for example. The transposition of ancient sun-hymnody to support the Israelite ideology of Torah would thus be the unique thrust of Psalm 19.

However, granted such a polemical basis as an *original* feature of this psalm, it is doubtful that such a motivation would be self-evident or of primary significance to those Israelites of later times who inherited it and prayed its words. Nor does such a historical observation exhaust the theological and literary meanings of Psalm 19, as shall be seen.

Part 3, moreover, has been presumptively assumed by most modern interpreters to be a late appendix to parts 1 and 2. But such an assessment overlooks the fact that part 3 shares considerable vocabulary with the earlier sections, and, more significantly, actually provides the religious-psychological motivation for the entire prayer. Rather than parts 1 and 2 serving polemical functions for the psalmist, a holistic view of the received psalm shows these subsections to provide both the prologue and the counterpoint to his request. His desire to be forgiven for covenantal transgressions is set within a larger praise of God as lawgiver and creator.

Taken altogether, Psalm 19 is a religious prayer whose various interlocking features appear under the aspect of speech. In part 1 the heavens and firmament speak; day and night speak; and sounds and words traverse the entirety of the created order. In part 2 the Torah of YHWH is a communication of divine laws and commandments: its words are the instructions of God to Israel. And, in part 3, the psalmist refers to his petition-prayer as the "words of my mouth," in contrast to the words of God's Torah and creation. Speech is, then, the root metaphor of this entire psalm.

Part 1 presents the world of creation engaged in unending speech: the heavens and firmament speak; day speaks to day; and night speaks to night. The psalmist thus conveys his sense of a harmonious creation which, in its day-to-day existence, "bespeaks" or "expresses" the glory of its creator. The creation is a testimonial to its creator, whose splendor is manifest everywhere in the world. There is no mention of man here, only the created elements of Genesis 1:1–2a which preceded him: the heavens and firmament, night and day, earth and sun. The language of praise is thus not human discourse but rather the rhythmic and mighty "language of creation" as it courses silently through time and space. There is neither "speech nor words—for their voice is not heard."

In this objective, impersonal section God is called El, which suggests a certain majestic austerity and contrasts with the sevenfold usage of the personal divine name YHWH in the succeeding sections, where the life of mankind is more directly engaged. We may recall that God was known as El to the patriarchs but as YHWH to Moses and all Israel in Egypt and thereafter (cf. Exodus 6).

Early rabbinic tradition often made an exegetical distinction between the uses of the divine names El-Elohim and YHWH. El was understood as indicative of the presence of God as a remote cosmic judge; YHWH, as suggestive of God's merciful presence.[3] While such an exegetical distinction is by no means consonant with a reading of the whole Bible, it does enrich our understanding of such narratives as Genesis 22 (The Binding of Isaac), and such psalms as Psalm 19. The praise of creation in the first part, then, is to El, the creator of nature. With part 2, man enters. Connecting God and man is the Torah of YHWH.

In this psalm, God is seen as both the Creator of harmonious nature and teacher of mankind through His Torah. In theological terms, part 1 deals with Creation, part 2 with Revelation. God the Creator relates more intimately with His creation through His revealed Torah. Creation praises God; Revelation teaches man. The scene thus shifts from heaven to earth. God's image shifts from a passive, praised Being to an active, teaching Presence.

From the human standpoint, which is the standpoint of prayer, the Revelation, the Torah of YHWH, is a new creation, giving order and harmony to the social cosmos. The Israelite community, called into existence by God's teachings, will praise Him by abiding by His teachings.

In part 2, all the ancient epithets of the sun and the righteous ruler appear with an emphasis on Torah: it is pure, upright, trustworthy, just, and life-sustaining. Man is enlightened, restored, and informed. Splendor and purity, steadfastness and justice, joy and wisdom come from the Torah. Its worth is more than gold. It is sweeter than the sap of the honeycomb. By fulfilling the Torah, man achieves his true end. The Torah is God's creation; those who live by it praise Him. As compared to part 1 and its harmonious, poetic lines, part 2 is made up of didactic, constructed prose. In part 1 nature is presented neutrally—it just "is." The didacticism of part 2, by contrast, is

tendentious and purposeful. With the Revelation, and God's
addressing presence, value enters and transforms the world of
nature. With Revelation, mankind finds an orientation of value
within the undifferentiated manifold of creation.

Revelation thus sharpens the focus of creation from the
human point of view. To transpose a rabbinic image: the ten
words by which the world was created (cf. *Ethics of the
Fathers*, V) are concretized and socialized in the ten words
spoken to the covenantal community in the Decalogue (Exodus
20). Revelation is the psalmist's access to God and creation; it is
also the way in which he—as Israelite—is singled out. Man
gives praise to God the Creator by fulfilling His will as
Revealer. Like all creatures of the creation, man has his proper
place. His creaturehood is expressed within the social community. The Torah is man's wisdom (Deuteronomy 4:6–8), and
through it he has a special relationship with God. Through
God's teachings man possesses hope for justice and righteous-
ness.

In part 3 the psalmist is fully subjective, as "your servant."
The praise of the preceding part now turns to pain; the
transition is verbally textured by the phrase: "Even your
servant is made resplendent [*nizhar*] by them." The reference
here is to the preceding Revelation of Torah-teachings and
their ordering, sustaining, and restorative power. The verb
nizhar, "is made resplendent," continues the metaphor of
luminosity and purity found in the previous two parts. But it
can also mean "is warned." This second meaning deepens the
connection between the psalmist's present cry and his foregoing praise of Torah. The focus is now on the observance of
the life-enhancing Torah of YHWH, as well as on the attendant
difficulties of religious servitude and obedience.

The psalmist now articulates his anxiety that—despite his
best intentions—his is not a pure relationship with God. For
"who can know unwitting faults?" The psalmist wants to be
cleared of "hidden" *(nistar)* errors. With this reference the
inner coherence of the prayer is further disclosed: for in part 1
nothing was "hidden" *(nistar)* from the sun's shine; and in part
2 the Torah, much like a sun, "enlightens" and makes "bright"
the social polity. The psalmist avers that he has tried to obey
the law and prays that he not be held responsible for what he
does unintentionally, without knowledge.

Part 3 also reveals that the psalmist senses himself in the

grip of compelling urges, of dominating drives. He does not merely request grace for ritual inadvertencies and alleviation from his anxiety. "May they not coerce [stem: *mashal*] me!" he states. This same verbal stem was used in the Cain and Abel narrative, when God told Cain that if he did well he could "withstand" or "dominate" the temptations to his will. The psalmist also knows that evil and error are not committed by ignorance alone. He knows that what might begin with an unintentional act often heaps up a pattern of behavior all the more insidious because disguised in the cloak of inadvertence. He asks God to help him that he may "be pure," even as the "Torah of YHWH is pure."

The psalmist fears errors against God and man; he fears actions which are hidden from him; he fears his own rebellious, unconscious will. With God's help, on which he can rely—for is not God the omnipotent Creator and beneficent Revealer?—he trusts that he will be protected from future iniquities. This is his hope, these are "the words of my mouth" to "YHWH, my rock and my redeemer."

The true subject of part 3 is, then, Redemption. The petition of the psalmist is addressed to God the Creator and Revealer of parts 1 and 2. The style shifts; the words of hope and need are disjunctive and anxious, as contrasted with the hymnic, parallel strophes of part 1 and the explicatory didacticisms of part 2. They express hesitant, anxious emotions. They burst from the soul and shatter the stately elegance of the language of the psalm's opening lines. The lines of part 3, by contrast, reveal the psalmist in his radical subjectivity, with his own torment and anxiety. The chasm between God's words of revelation and man's corresponding acts are bridged by the words and act of prayer. The psalmist is revealed as a creature in need of redemption.

What the psalmist gives to God are his words, his prayer, his praise of the creation and the teachings of the Torah. These words set the context of hope and elicit the confidence to conquer the despair of his present situation. Nature reveals God the Creator, the Torah reveals God's will, but the prayer of the lonely soul reveals man's presence and situation. The psalmist turns to God his Redeemer in a trust confirmed and affirmed by the realities expressed in the earlier verses. He asks God to hear both his outer words and inner thoughts which he hopes will find favorable acceptance *(ratzon)* before Him, much as a sacrifice might.

David, in his broken torment after killing Uriah and taking his wife Bathsheba, voices a similar hope:

> Save me from revenge, Elohim, God of my deliverance,
>   and I shall shout abroad Your justice.
> Open my lips, my Lord,
>   that my mouth bespeak Your praise.
> Indeed, You desire not a sacrifice,
>   and if I brought* an offering you'd not accept [*tirtzeh*] it.
> The sacrifices of Elohim are a broken spirit.
>   Elohim, do not despise a broken and crushed heart!
>
> (Psalm 51:16–19)

The whole of Psalm 19 thus turns on the offering of words and the request for divine favor in the concluding line. The possibility that the psalmist's words will not be favorable to God is the silent abyss which opens up within the hope of the petition. Indeed, no direct answer from God is found in this prayer. All we have are the psalmist's words: words of praise and hope; words of struggle for spiritual integrity before God. And yet it is the mystery inherent in the process of prayer that an answer is, in fact, given; it is an answer expressed in and through the very capacity of the psalmist to voice his anxiety. The grace of a petition-prayer is the gift of hope received in the very process of its recitation.

---

*I understand *ve'etanah* as the cohortative *ve'etenah*, and do not follow the Massoretic punctuation.

7. Jeremiah 20:7–12 / Loneliness and Anguish

(7) You have enticed me, YHWH, and I've been had:
  You have overwhelmed me and prevailed;
    I am mocked all day long,
    Everyone reviles me.

(8) Whenever I speak or shout, I cry: "violence and plunder!"—
    The word of YHWH is become my daily shame and
      reproach.

(9) And whenever I would think: "I won't mention Him,
    Nor speak in His name ever again"—
    Then His word burned me up like a consuming fire locked in
      my bones;
    I have tried to contain it but to no avail.

(10) Surely I have heard the slander of many—terror on every
      side:
    "Let us denounce him but good!"
    Even old friends and sidekicks have said:
    "Perhaps he may be enticed—then we'll prevail against
      him
    And get our revenge!"

(11) But YHWH is with me like a mighty warrior,
    Therefore my pursuers shall stumble and not prevail;
    They shall be sorely abashed for lack of success,
    With an unforgettable, permanent shame.

(12) O YHWH of Hosts, who tests the righteous and sees the
      innermost heart,
    Let me see Your revenge on them—
    For I have revealed my case to You.

Jeremiah 20:7–12 is one of many lay prayers in the Hebrew Bible not found in the Book of Psalms. A common feature of these prayers is their spontaneous character and immediate relationship to a situation of personal crisis. Indeed, in contradistinction to the first-person laments recited in ancient Israelite shrines (e.g., Psalms 7; 28; 35; 109), first-person laments not found in the Psalter (like the prayer of Jonah) are inextricably linked to a specific individual. Thus, however much a later idealization of Jeremiah's suffering may have

affected the editorial decision to include Jeremiah's private
prayers in a collection of his public oracles—with the result
that these prayers could become spiritually paradigmatic for
others in similar situations—the relationship between Jeremiah 20:7-12 and the prophet himself is primary.[1] Every effort
must therefore be made to locate the singular characteristics
of Jeremiah 20:7-12 within Jeremiah's life history as a
messenger of God.

But it is just here that a number of problems confront the
latter-day interpreter. What indications does the text provide
for a precise historical ascription? At first glance, there
appears to be a historical and situational relation between
20:7-12 and the preceding scenario in 20:1-6, where Jeremiah
is described as having been physically abused by his enemies
after a prophetic denunciation; there is, moreover, a specific
phraseological link between these two passages. Jeremiah's
oracle against his persecutor Pashhur (vv.3-4) pivots on a
reinterpretation of the latter's name as *magor missaviv*,
"terror on every side," an expression used by Jeremiah in v.10
to characterize his own distress. But, despite these conjunc-
tions, any actual nexus between the events of vv.1-6 and the
prayer of vv.7-12 is not certain. In fact, it is more likely that it
reflects a secondary, redactional conceit. This assumption is
reinforced by what appears to be an editorial doubling-up of
prayers in 20:7-18; for the somewhat hopeful conclusion
reached in the first prayer (vv.7-12) is immediately undercut
by the suicidal cry of anguish in the second (vv.14-18). Given
these considerations, and the fact that 20:7-12 presents
Jeremiah's plight as something recurrent in his biography, it
may be prudent to approach the prayer as a heightened
expression of Jeremiah's inner history as a prophet of God, and
not feel constrained to locte its precise setting in life.

The foregoing methodological difficulty—that of finding in
Jeremiah 20:7-12 textual indicators sufficient to establish its
historical locus—has its corollary in the difficulty of finding
in Jeremiah's prayer formal directives fully adequate to a
confident understanding of its inner logic and progression. As
the received prayer is full of obscure or missing connections
between phrases (8*a*, *b*, and *c*) and among units (v.10 and vv.11-
12), an interpreter is constantly required to make sense of its
syntactic ambiguities.

And because Jeremiah 20:7-12 is now a literary artifact—a

canonical transcription of a spoken event—no audible tones or breath sequences linger to inspire exegetical confidence. What will be produced, by way of interpretation, is a reflex of the dialectical relationship between Jeremiah 20:7-12 and one reader; what will be achieved is but one public testimony of the inner life of this prayer as resurrected—through an interior recitative performance of it—by one interpreter.

Jeremiah's words are addressed to God: tormented by his enemies, he feels anger and accusation, betrayal and hope commingled in him. The experiences and consequences of his prophetic destiny are "revealed" as a "case" *(riv)* before the Lord. In his vulnerability Jeremiah turns to God, and says: *"You."* This language of direct encounter frames the prayer, bracketing and counterpointing the references to God as "Him" and "He," and the citations of the enemies' plots against "him" (Jeremiah). Such rapid shifts of subject and object, and of other-directed and self-directed address, constitute one of several stylistic features in Jeremiah 20:7-12.

The general ring structure to the prayer, just indicated, may be more fully delineated:

A stanza 1 (v.7) direct speech to God ("You")

B stanza 2 (vv.8-9) self-reflection; indirect reference to God ("He")

C stanza 3 (v.10) recollection of enemies' plots against "him"

B' stanza 4 (v.11) self-reflection; indirect reference to "the Lord"

A' stanza 5 (v.12) direct speech to God ("You")

This chiastic form also serves to diagram the inner transformations of Jeremiah 20:7-12. The framing stanzas (A and A') address God directly, whereas the internal ones move on a more reflective plane and incorporate the "case" presented to God. These internal stanzas are not, however, of a piece. Stanzas 2 and 3 develop the claims put forward in stanza 1, whereas stanza 4 is separated from 1-3 in terms of mood, theme, and tense: the speaker returns to the present moment and switches from balanced lines to an extended prose assertion. The bursting forth of hope in stanzas 4 and 5 confirm the force of God's presence upon the prophet referred to in the opening sections. In a sense, stanzas 1-3 are Jeremiah's attempt to restrain the words of prophecy and release the tensions he feels by means of a protest-prayer directed to God. But the shift towards hope in stanzas 4-5 indicates that God's presence could not be long suppressed in him, and that prophetic words would again burst forth from Jeremiah's lips.

The entire prayer moves from despair to hopeful assertion; from psychical disintegration to spiritual wholeness. As Jeremiah's sense of destiny and vocation are restored in the course of his prayer, a growing confidence emerges. Indeed, Jeremiah 20:7-12 is a verbal record of a religious sufferer who is transformed in and through the language of his prayer, offered to God for His judgment and verdict.

The first unit of Jeremiah 20:7-12, v.7, opens the prayer with an expression of anger and impotence. Jeremiah accuses God of having taken unfair advantage of him; *pittitaniy*, he says, *va'efat*, "You have enticed me...and I've been had": *hizaqtaniy vattukhal*, "You have overwhelmed me and prevailed" (v.7a). This incriminating broadside seems to point beyond specific moments in Jeremiah's life as a prophet and include the very roots of his prophetic destiny, concerning which two levels can be distinguished: Jeremiah was foreordained by God to be a prophet while yet in the womb (1:4), and was confirmed in this destiny upon reaching majority (vv.5-8). In his present protest (20:7), which refers to his ineluctable fate, Jeremiah undoubtedly felt, on the one hand, that God took unfair advantage of him before his will was formed; and that he had also been beguiled by God against his conscious—though timid—will, for God had told him not to fear, saying: "I will be with you to protect you....I have made you forthwith as a protected fortress, a pillar of bronze, and walls of iron; [people] will contend against you, but they will not prevail [*lo'yukhlu lakh*]" (1:8, 18).

Jeremiah felt that all such blandishments of support had proved worthless. For if his curse of his birth day in 20:14-18 most fully expresses his anger at this prenatal destiny, vv. 7-10 most fully indict God for leading him on time after time, such that he suffered persecutions for His sake. As if to provide a physical correlative to his sense of being "forced," Jeremiah expresses himself by means of terms (*pittitaniy*, You have enticed me"; *hizaqtaniy*, "You have overwhelmed me") which elsewhere refer to sexual seduction and rape (see Exodus 22:15

and Deuteronomy 22:25, respectively).[2] It is furthermore striking that in Ezekiel 14:9 a true prophet is described as one who is *yefutteh*, induced or set upon, to speak the word of God; and that in 1 Kings 22:22 the true prophet Micaihu reports his vision wherein God instructed an evil spirit to speak lies through the mouths of the prophets of King Jehoshaphat with the words: *tefatteh vegam tukhal*, "You will traduce and prevail." These several interpenetrating overtones of the verb *pittah* were conceivably present to Jeremiah's consciousness as he voiced his protest; they nevertheless permit the modern interpreter, aware of such a developed semantic field for this verb, a fuller sympathetic penetration into the conflicting feelings which ravaged Jeremiah's heart. Accordingly, on the basis of the implicit semantics of *pittah*, the prophet is felt to be a person at once overwhelmed by God's control and filled with an acute sense of having been duped by Him—for Jeremiah goes on (in v.7b) to describe his life as a prophet as an unbroken series of torments.

The relationship between v.7a and v.7b is cumulative. Jeremiah's opening outburst about the impact of divine power over him is concretized in the succeeding depiction of his victimization at human hands. For the prophet, a void of anguish lies between the pressure of divine power and the pain of human scorn; indeed, the net effect of the second clause (v.7b) is to strip the earlier references to divine power (v.7a) of any providential dimension. Jeremiah feels possessed and abandoned.

What has collapsed for Jeremiah is his trust in God's promised protection. How is God a bulwark for him in the face of such daily disdain? As the contempt of the community to whom he speaks invades his soul, and as he senses the collapse of his inner strength, Jeremiah believes God to be absent from him and cries out in despair and protest. True, others in similar circumstances found solace in memories of divine care:

> Woe, I'm a worm and not a man,
> Shamed by men and condemned by the crowd;
> Whosoever sees me, reviles me...
> But You it was who guided my bursting forth at birth,
> Who placed me trustingly at my mother's breasts.
> I've been cast before You since birth;
> From my mother's womb You are my God. (Psalm 22:7-8,10)

Not so Jeremiah, who felt himself doubly deceived: before

birth he was conditioned with a God-given destiny, and from adolescence on (cf. 15:20) he was beguiled by God and His promised protection.

The next section of Jeremiah's prayer, vv.8-9, deepens the opening verse and extends its thrust. Detailed reflections replace and justify the initial charge. Verse 8 (victimization by men) develops v.7*b*, and v.9 (vulnerability before God) develops v.7*a*, thereby replicating on a smaller scale the chiastic structure of the prayer as a whole. In v.8 Jeremiah reports his case to God: how he rebuked the people for injustice and violence—but himself became a victim; how he exposed the plunder roundabout and spoke the prophetic "word of YHWH." The tone is despairing and indignant. The prophet focuses on the personal consequences of his words, and speaks resentfully of his task. In fact, internal ambiguities in the syntax of v.8 give this resentment an unexpected irony. For when Jeremiah cries "violence and plunder" it is unclear whether he is exposing the injustice of his fellowmen, or whether he is reacting to the violence done to him as a result of his speaking and shouting.[3] A recent opinion has even proposed that the sense of v.8 is that whenever Jeremiah *shouts* prophetic words to the people he *cries* to God for the *violence* which He has done to him in forcing him to speak.[4] All this and more; for it is even possible that the syntax of the opening phrases in v.8 must not be construed "whenever I speak or shout, I cry: 'violence and plunder!'"—but: "whenever I speak, I shout, and cry." Such a reading effectively and rhythmically underscores the fitful nature of Jeremiah's prophetic speech. But while the network of syntactic ambiguity in v.8 is truly complex, there does not seem to be any necessity to affirm one resolution at the expense of another. Indeed, such rich ambiguity suggests simultaneous levels of protest and distress raging within Jeremiah, each one struggling for life expression.

As remarked earlier, v.9 extends the issues of v.7*a*. Jeremiah's constant speaking (*middey 'addaber*, v.8) of the prophetic word *(dabar)* is juxtaposed to the decision not to speak *(lo' 'addaber*, v.9) God's words again. The rabble reviled him with contempt and frightened him with plots; they conspired that "his name [*shemo*] would never be mentioned [*yizzaker*] again" (11:19). As a result, Jeremiah thought to reject his task, to refuse to "mention Him [*'ezkarennu*]" or "speak in His name [*shemo*] ever again." But this was impossible. He could not banish God's controlling voice within him. Even within the very course of this brief protest, the prophet is constrained to admit: "I have tried to contain [*kalkel*] (God's word) but to no avail [*velo' 'ukhal*]." The verbal and thematic link with v.7a ("You have overwhelmed me and prevailed [*vattukhal*]") is obvious. Indeed, the reemployment of the same verbal stem serves to dramatize Jeremiah's spiritual crisis. He can neither reject his task nor control his fate *(velo' 'ukhal)*; whereas God is fully and forcefully in control *(vattukhal)* of him.

Comparable portrayals of the internal and physical dimensions of prophetic experience are found elsewhere in the Book of Jeremiah. At an earlier point in his life, Jeremiah knew that he was unable to withhold God's words of doom. He felt the need to speak them long before they broke the barrier of his lips:

> O my pain, my deep, inward pain!
> My heart bursts its walls,
> My being strains and breaks.
> I cannot keep silent. (4:19–20)

Now, again, Jeremiah is filled with the unyielding prophetic word of "fire" (*'esh* v.9), an image he elsewhere used to distinguish the force of authentic prophetic speech from the slick-styled lingo of prophetic pretenders: "For is not my word [*devariy*] like fire [*'esh*], oracle of YHWH, like a hammer smashing stone?" (Jeremiah 23:29). The true prophet, he stresses, is consumed by the scorching power of his uncontainable task, and bellows forth words which sear the security of the nation. "Behold," said God to Jeremiah, in a rephrasing of the commission language of 1:9, "I am making My words [*devaray*] in your mouth as fire [*'esh*]; and this people are like wood which it will consume!" (5:14). "Can grain be compared to chaff?" (23:28)—even so can the self-induced fantasies of false prophets replace the true Word of God.

> My heart has crashed within me,
> All my bones sway;
> I am like a drunkard,
> Soaked with wine—
> Because of YHWH,
> Because of His holy words! (23:9)

Thus Jeremiah knew himself seduced and filled by divine words of fire (20:9). Much as his frequent wish that he had died unborn in his mother's womb (15:10; 20:14-18) is undisguised anger at the natural source of his destiny, his present attempt to stifle the prophetic word incubating within him is, correspondingly, an attempt to act out this anger on his own body. Perhaps because of the prenatal (1:5) and adolescent (1:9; 5:14) factors in his prophetic biography, Jeremiah recurrently expressed his experiences with images of interiority (e.g., 4:19--20; 15:10, 15-16; 20:9, 14-18; 23:9).[5]

He knew in his "bones" that he could not reject his prophetic destiny. But he could not accept it, either. And so, just here lay Jeremiah's tragic paradox. Like Thamyris of old, Jeremiah was hounded by divine demands. But when Thamyris tried to inhibit his inspiring divine voices, the gods crippled him with a more awesome silence (*Iliad*, 2:594-600). Jeremiah, by contrast, could not for a moment restrain the divine words which consumed him. He felt himself—in the mocking words once spoken by the Muses about their prophetic mediums—a wretched thing of shame, a mere belly.[6]

Verse 10 deepens the reality of Jeremiah's torment. The mocking and derision referred to in vv.7*b* and 8*b* is now fully expressed through two quotes. The prophet presents new evidence of his "case," of his being a constantly reviled messenger. Jeremiah tells God how he has heard the scheming of his enemies: they hope to trick him and do him in; they have encircled him—"terror on every side" *(magor missaviv)*.

Several elements in Jeremiah's characterization of his enemies' threats against him have ironic resonances. It will be recalled that the phrase "terror on every side" picks up the language of Jeremiah 20:3-4, where Jeremiah told Pashur that he would henceforth be called *magor missaviv* (v.3)—for God would bring "terror," *magor*, "upon you and all your compatriots." Since Jeremiah has also used this phrase to announce the invasion of the enemy who would actualize the divine punishment against Israel (6:22-25), his present use of it to express his own sense of personal *magor* (20:20) underscores the irony of Jeremiah's prayer in relation to his oracles, and his sense of being a victim of attack and siege. Additionally, when Jeremiah remarks that his enemies have plotted against him, and cites them as saying: "Perhaps he may be enticed [*yefutteh*]—then we'll prevail [*nukhlah*] against him," his words echo those spoken by Jeremiah to God at the outset of the prayer *(pittiytaniy...vattukhal)*. This intratextual loop, whereby Jeremiah's victimization by God and man is captured in identical language, adds additional irony to the protest, and suggests a structural analogy between Jeremiah and the patriarch Jacob. Jacob contended with God and man and prevailed (*vattukhal*, Genesis 32:29), whereas Jeremiah struggled with God and men, but was prevailed over by both. This is the deep anguish of his situation.

But now a change occurs. Without warning, the prayer shifts gears (vv.11-12). Just what has been implicit throughout— namely, Jeremiah's inescapable commitment to God—is now made explicit. With renewed confidence the prophet affirms: "But YHWH is with me like a mighty warrior." The negative, recriminatory tone of the opening stanzas is abruptly replaced by this positive assertion of divine providence, as much hoped for as experienced. With this shift in mood, it would seem that Jeremiah has regained his composure, and that the crisis of confidence has been abated. Picking up on the enemies' hope to prevail against him (*nukhlah*, v.10), Jeremiah rejoices that his enemies will no longer prevail (*yukhalu*, v.11). This recurrence of the verb "to prevail" reminds us that each stanza of the prayer has used variations on the stem *yakhal* ("to be able"; "prevail"), such that it underlines the thematic transformations and progressions in Jeremiah 20:7-12 as a whole. Seen thus, the prayer moves from God's power over Jeremiah, and Jeremiah's corresponding impotence, to the enemies' will for power over Jeremiah, and his corresponding spiritual triumph.

The thematic significance of the stem *yakhal* in Jeremiah 20:7-12 is complemented by tonal dimensions, as well. The phonemes /k-l/, together with the allophonic variations /g-l/ and /q-l/, produce an alliterative network of sounds which thicken and unify the intensity of the prayer[7] Accordingly, diverse verbs and nouns are coordinated on the basis of their euphony with the root stem *yakhal*. In this way the tone of struggle inherent in the key verb prevails throughout the prayer, as the following transcription makes clear:

v. 7...*vattuKhaL hayitiy LetzhoQ KoL hayyom KuLLoh Lo'eG Liy*

v. 8...*hayah...Liy Leherpa uLeQeLes KoL hayyom*

v. 9...*niL'etiy KaLKeL veLo' 'uKhaL*

v.10...*Kiy...KoL..'uLay yeffutteh venuKhLah Lo veniQuah niQmatenu*

v.11...'*aL Ken..yiKashLu veLo' yuKhaLu..Kiy Lo'*
        hisKiLu KeLimmat 'oLam Lo'...
v.12...*bohen KeLayot vaLev..Kiy 'eLeKha GiLLiytiy 'et*
        riviy

The preceding does not exhaust the alliterations found in
Jeremiah 20:7-12, but it does underscore its prevalent to-
nalities.[8]

However, attentiveness to the phonemic sonority of Jeremiah's prayer does more than underscore its tonal unity or
orchestrate new combinations of its dominant thematic stem
(yakhal). It also enables one to shift critical attention away
from the representational character of speech and towards
nonrepresentational aspects of language—most pertinently, to
the relationships between sound, sense, and silence.[9] In the
process, a reader becomes a listener, sensitive to and appreciative of the way silences create or modulate linguistic meaning.
As a "speechless want" (Merleau-Ponty) gives birth to tones
rhythmically deployed, "enjambements" of sound clusters and
silence presume to express a speaker's heart and mind—and
just this is the paradox and miracle of speech. For speech
organizes the swirl of indiscriminate sounds and silence, and
creates a world—a cosmos—with words. But when, however,
these resonant tones—inspired and animated by human
breath—fade into a new silence, the same speaker is now left
with but the echo of his hopes. Sensitivity to these dialectics of
sound, sense, and silence deepens our literary and human
appreciation of Jeremiah's prayer. For this prayer is not only a
heightened expression of linguistic dynamics generally, but
comments on a dialectic of sound and silence all the more
awesome: the word of God in the resisting heart of man.

But although Jeremiah 20:7-12 has a tonal and linguistic
unity, the sharp transition from v.10 to v.11 still begs explanation.[10] What explains the abrupt transition from Jeremiah's remonstrations of injustice to his assurance that God
will judge justly? A double process may have been at work. On
the one hand, we have noted that the language of Jeremiah's
restatement of the plots of his enemies: "Perhaps he may be
enticed [*yefutteh*]—then we'll prevail [*nukhlah*] against him"
(v.10), harks back to his opening protest that God had enticed
him *(pittiytaniy)* and prevailed *(tukhal)*. While these references to being enticed reinforce the sense of victimization
which pervades the prayer, they may also have had a

dialectical effect. Jeremiah was presumably stimulated to realize that such domination was also a sign of God's presence in the life of a true prophet (cf. 23:9, 29). Such a realization would serve to restore Jeremiah's confidence in his task. "YHWH is with me," he exults, "like a mighty warrior."

Repetitions of the verbal stem *yakhal* may also have helped trigger Jeremiah's inner transformation. Not only could the sense of being prevailed upon have produced a reaction similar to the foregoing, but the stem *yakhal* could also have served to remind Jeremiah of God's promise of protection in his original commission to prophecy:

> And they will contend against you, but will not prevail *(lo' yukhlu)* against you; for I am with *('et)* you, oracle of YHWH, to save you. (1:10)

Thereby reconfirmed in his destiny, Jeremiah boldly took up the words of this promise in his exultation and wish: "YHWH is with [*'et*] me," he shouts; but as for his enemies, let their fate be as promised long ago: *lo' yukhalu*, "let them not prevail" (v.11).

However, while Jeremiah 20:11 (stanza 4) does reflect the prophet's new resolve, it does not conclude the prayer. Closure is found in v.12 (stanza 5), where the successive alliterations of the preceding verses *(k/g-l)* reecho with a "summative" effect: *ro'eh KeLayot vaLev...Kiy 'eLeKha GiLLiytiy 'et riviy.* At first glance Jeremiah's appeal for divine revenge against his enemies merely serves to pull together the preceding charges of injustice. But, in fact, the conclusion completes the transformation of Jeremiah's religious consciousness begun in v.11. The prophet speaks to God as one who "tests [*bohen*] the righteous [*tzadiq*]." Such a phrase is an ironic reversal of Jeremiah's God-appointed task as a "tester" (*bahon*; cf. 6:27). It also reflects Jeremiah's revised perception regarding his suffering. He does not refer to God as a righteous *(tzedeq)* judge or tester—in continuity with his own and other biblical expressions—but as the One who tests him, Jeremiah, who is *tzadiq*: a justified or righteous person. Jeremiah has presumably come to realize that his torment is but a test, and that he has never been abandoned. He therefore trusts in God's avenging justice against his enemies.

And yet, Jeremiah's new personal truth—which retrospectively annihilates his past pain as something wrongly seen—raises new questions. If God put His own word in Jeremiah's

heart (*libbiy*, v.9), and can "see" *(ro'eh)* the innermost heart
(lev) of man (v.12), what need be there for testing? And
further, what need be there for Jeremiah to reveal his case to
Him whose knowledge comprehends all?

The logic of such a closure to this prayer would thus seem to
undermine its very pathos and necessity. But not entirely. For
it is in the very process of prayer that the prophet has achieved
his new knowledge. What Jeremiah achieves by revealing his
case to God is to see his life in a new way. In the process, he
recognizes himself as a tested sufferer—one whose physical
and emotional torment does not invalidate the divine promise
of protective providence. God's protection is spiritualized; it is
the confidence He gives His servants that their heart and
service are seen and accepted. This realization, as the others,
would seem to underlie the transition from despair to hope in
vv.11-12. Jeremiah's final appeal for violent recrimination
against his enemies reflects his new confidence with all the
venom of *resentment*: You "who *sees* the innermost heart, let me
see Your revenge..."

This remarkable prayer reveals a tragic moment wherein a
prophet despairs but cannot fully rebel. Jeremiah struggles to
suppress God's voice within him. But his realization that God's
word is in his bones, and his recognition of divine protection in
v.11, point to the reunification of his will with God's. Jeremiah's spiritual restoration lies in the full acceptance of his
unique task in the world: to be a faithful and trusting divine
messenger.

No word of God comes to build or confirm Jeremiah's hope
and confidence, as happens elsewhere (11:21-23, 12:5-6; 15:19-
21). But we know, nevertheless, that Jeremiah will again speak
in His name; for he quickly added—or are these the words of
another?—the following hymn (v.13):

> Sing to YHWH;
> Praise YHWH;
> For He has saved a needy soul from his enemies!

8. Psalm 122 / Space in Suspension: The Pilgrimage

A Song of Ascents, by David:

> I rejoiced when they said to me: "Let us go to the Temple of YHWH."
>
> Our feet were standing in your gates, O Jerusalem.
> Jerusalem: built like a city in which all is joined in unity.
>
> For there the tribes had all ascended—
> Tribes of YH, a testimony to Israel—
> To acknowledge the name of YHWH.
> For there were found seats of justice,
> The seats of the dynasty of David.
>
> "Beseech the peace of Jerusalem [and say]:
> 'May those who love you find repose;
> Let peace pervade your turrets,
> And repose fill your battlements.'"
>
> For the sake of my brethren and friends,
> I shall bespeak your peace;
> For the sake of the Temple of YHWH, Our God,
> I shall beseech you all good.

Psalm 122 opens with the superscription: *Shir Ha-ma'alot le-David*, "A Song of Ascents, by David." But whether these "ascents"—which introduce Psalms 120–34 as well—refer to musical notations, the arrangement of choristers on the Temple stairs (as they were in fact deployed during the time of the second Temple), or the ascension of a pilgrimage, is no longer certain. Nevertheless, the fact that the content of this psalm is clearly concerned with pilgrims to Jerusalem, and also refers to the ascension *('alu)* of the tribes in the third stanza, suggests the third alternative for the meaning of *ma'alot* ("ascents") to be the one most likely in the present case.

Although this particular prayer has been transmitted as part of a communal songbook, a profoundly personal reality pervades its words. It is a prayer-offering, a shout of joy, made by one who has been transformed into a member of a religious fellowship. It is, in fact, his recollection of that transformative moment in his life.

The psalm begins with an "I-in-isolation" ("*I* rejoiced") called to a communal task by a group "we" ("Let *us*"). The speaker is invited to join a collective action, to become a pilgrim. With this opening shift from the individual to the collective, the verbs of the psalm undergo a corresponding shift: all are in the plural until the final praises and blessings. Only at the end of the prayer does the personal voice of the speaker return ("*I* shall bespeak....*I* shall beseech"). But he is now an "I" strengthened through communal sharing, an "I" qualitatively different from the single one who was called out of his singular and isolated existence to "go to the Temple."

References to the "Temple of YHWH" frame this psalm: they occur in the opening invitation of the friends ("Let us go to the Temple of YHWH") and in the closing blessing of the speaker ("For the sake of the Temple of YHWH")—a fact which reminds us that the Temple of Jerusalem is the physical and spiritual center of the entire prayer; indeed, its existence explains both the pilgrims' motivation for action and their shared focus.

This collective anticipation of, and orientation to, worship in the Temple was and remains so dominant in the psalmist's consciousness that his recollection of the actual journey is totally compressed. The transition from the invocatory "Let us," spoken in the periphery, prior to the act of pilgrimage, to the report, "Our feet were standing in your gates, O Jerusalem," spoken at the center, at the spatial focus of the pilgrimage, is immediate. They are the first two spoken breaths of the psalm; the one an exhalation outward, the other an inhalation and ingathering of energy. In their juxtaposition, the hope and the reality are fused; the journey and its terrors are ignored. The way has been traversed—but without comment.

Jerusalem was the sacred center, the space of the Temple of the Lord of all Israel. It was the "city of Elohim" (Psalm 46:5), the "splendor of the earth" (Psalm 48:3). When Solomon dedicated the shrine in Jerusalem, blessing and justice were promised to the people. Even in exile an Israelite could orient himself to the Temple and call down the riches of heaven and forgiveness (1 Kings 8). "For YHWH has chosen Zion, He has desired it for His place of [earthly] habitation" (Psalm 132:13). God loves Jerusalem more than all the dwellings of Jacob (Psalm 87:2); she is, in fact, the physical and spiritual mother of the people (vv.5–6).

Years later, the central royal shrine of Solomon in Jerusalem became the one and only place of legitimate worship for all Israelites (Deuteronomy 12). It was only here that the ancient agricultural festivals of Passover, Ingathering, and Tabernacles were celebrated (Deuteronomy 15–16); and it was only here that the first fruits and freewill donations were brought, in repayment for past sustenance and in hopes of future beneficence on the land promised to the fathers (Deuteronomy 26). Perhaps this desire to seek the face of the Lord in Jerusalem with gifts of thanks is the life setting for this psalm. Or perhaps it is to the new postexilic Jerusalem, with its rebuilt and fortified walls, that the psalmist has been invited.

At all events, the psalmist knows the spiritual centrality of Jerusalem full well. It is, indeed, just this reality which has sustained him and his fellow travelers on their way. Jerusalem is a "thou" to whom he speaks intimately ("*your* gates, O Jerusalem"). He knows Jerusalem to be the center of his longing and movement, and not his alone. For all the tribes have come "to acknowledge the name of YHWH." In Jerusalem there is a renewal of fellow-feeling, of shared historical destiny. The dislocations of dispersion are made whole in the sacred center. Private grievances are transformed by the hopes for justice here (stanza 3), for Jerusalem is the seat of Davidic power and covenantal justice.

The comment in the second stanza, "Jerusalem: built like a city in which all is joined in unity," is mysterious, even obscure. Is it a later editorial aside, or is it, in truth, a reflection of the psalmist now praising Jerusalem? Standing "in your gates," the goal of his wandering, the psalmist cannot help but see in them a concrete expression of the unity he now feels with the community of pilgrims. For the psalmist is now "joined in unity" to their goal, their hopes, their memories. Can we not appreciate this remark as an exclamation of joy reflecting his newly won sense of a spiritual community? On the one hand, the psalmist's reflections move from the physical solidity of Jerusalem to the spiritual solidarity of those who stand in her gates; on the other, his joy at communal unity allows him to appreciate the fastness of the walls of this city of longing. He knows that its unity depends on the reunion of the tribes and that its exercise of justice constitutes its true strength.

But all these thoughts are, he implies, abruptly broken by the invocation reported in stanza 4 ("Beseech..."). While standing before the gates of Jerusalem the psalmist is called "out" of his reflections and revery by the words of the gatekeeper.[1] Throughout the biblical period prophets and judges sat at the gates of Jerusalem instructing and admonishing the people. Liturgies of entrance to the Temple are also known.[2] Often, it would appear, pilgrims were greeted by the kind of rhetorical question and ensuing answer found in Psalm 24:

> Who may ascend *(ya'aleh)* to the mountain of YHWH?. . .
> He who has clean hands and a pure heart,
> Who has not foresworn to falsehood or iniquity (vv.3-4).

A more expanded list of requirements, similar to the Decalogue, is enumerated in Psalm 15. The gatekeeper in Psalm 128, another "song of ascents," clearly states that one who fears the Lord and follows His ways will merit the blessings and bounty of Jerusalem always. Such blessings were also extended by priests to pilgrims in Psalms 118:26 and 129:8.

The difference between these invocatory blessings and Psalm 122 is that in the latter it is the pilgrim himself who is told by the gatekeeper, "Beseech the peace [*shalom*] of Jerusalem [*Yerushalayim*]"; it is the pilgrim who is informed how to bless the city. And this he determines to do in stanza 5, with a determination that is both a proclamation of commitment and an assertion of hope. Peace is proclaimed over Jerusalem "for the sake of my brethren and friends"—his new brethren who have shared this journey, and his friends who are still at home. The peace of Jerusalem is proclaimed for the new brotherhood, present round about him; and it is proclaimed for all whose hearts are directed to the Temple of the Lord, wherever their bodies dwell. All Israel is one fellowship, and peace is proclaimed for those near and far.

With these concluding words, "for the sake of my brethren," the speaker regains and reasserts his "I," but with a profoundly transformed sense of self. The psalmist is no longer the separate "I" led into collective action by a vague ensemble of people going up to Jerusalem. He is now an "I" whose sense of self has been interwoven with the life of his fellows. He has shared with them, physically and spiritually. He speaks of them in familial terms and incorporates them into his blessing. He turns confidently to the future ("I *shall* bespeak"), knowing that this moment of decision, arising from a shared past, will continue beyond the present moment in the shrine and will generate a new life commitment. The shrine is now not simply referred to as the "Temple of the Lord," as in the opening line, but, significantly, as "the Temple of the Lord, *Our God*." Indeed, the very recitation of this psalm after the occasion of pilgrimage is itself confirmation of the psalmist's transformation and new dedication. It constitutes a verbal offering of memory and witness.

Motifs and Other Text-Transformations

9. The "Eden" Motif / The Landscape of Spatial Renewal

The notion of the shrine as a sacred place of renewal, discussed in the preceding chapter, is related to a mythic image that is widespread among world religions and those of the ancient Near East in particular; namely, that the creation began at and unfolded from a specific center point. This primal place was regarded as the paradigm of all origins, the point where heaven and earth met. Imagined as a "world mountain," it symbolized order, harmony, and beneficence. Sacred trees with magical power were rooted there, and the earth exploded in physical luxury around four streams, marking off the ancient quadrants of the created world.[1]

In the Bible, it is the imagery of the garden of Eden which expresses this primordial mythograph. This imagery of Eden wends its way through the times and places of Israelite history, and can best be viewed in a series of texts which share common characteristics but which represent no coherent or integrated arrangement.[2] The persistence of this imagery suggests its significance for the ancient Israelites, even as its recurrence lends the Bible a measure of coherence.[3]

A "reading" of the Bible through the refracted shapes which this archetypal intuition of spatial harmony has assumed sponsors a unique mode of literary inquiry. For it regards the Bible not simply as composite textual phenomena, but as a closed system of texts; thus: a "text" of special status. Accordingly, whatever coherence is effected by the recurrence of words or motifs in single texts and composite narrative cycles—such as those explored in earlier chapters—a similar but more intriguing coherence is effected when the frame of reference is the entire Hebrew Bible. Indeed, by tracing the recurrent recomposition of Eden-imagery around core moments in biblical history, a unique dimension of that history is brought into view. For just as these imagistic representations of natural harmony provide symbolic vectors to those trans-natural intuitions which preceded them, so will attentiveness to the historical oscillations of Eden-imagery disclose the coordinates of a deep and persistent religious reality in the Bible. Put differently, the exegetical alignment of Eden-imagery in diverse biblical texts manifests a latent form of intertextual coherence which, reciprocally, transfigures our very understanding of the Bible-as-a-whole.

The Garden of Eden, the first home of mankind, is the archetypal expression of the experience of sacred geography in the Bible.[4] It is comprised of various components, which appear in Genesis 2-3:

1. Eden is located on a mountain, a *mountain of God*—a designation not explicitly stated in Genesis 2:4bff., although Eden's elevation is suggested through the fact of downward coursing streams. Eden is, however, characterized as a mountain in Ezekiel 28:13, where this motif is used to satirize the King of Tyre's pretensions to divinity.[5]

2. This mountain is a center point in the cosmos of creation, a place where heaven and earth, God and man, meet.

3. At the center of the mountain is a *garden*, in whose own center are two magical trees containing the secrets of life and knowledge.

4. From this garden rises a *stream* which flows, as from a navel, to the cosmic *quadrants*, thereby sustaining the earth.

The Garden of Eden is the symbol of all good—birth and blessing, life and knowledge, order and communication—which can be found on earth. Set in the primordial past, this Eden imagery reflects a memory of human harmony on earth, and so nurtures hope for its restoration.

With the dislocation from Eden, however, and the cursed entrance of mankind into history and its fatalities, the coherent symbolic configuration found in Genesis 2-3 shatters and decomposes into its several elements. The shards of Eden are, it will be recalled, reassembled in an ironic manner by the builders of the Tower of Babel. Their achievement serves as the paradigmatic antitype of Eden, exemplary of the misguided works of a mankind ever scurrying around the bricks on the plain of Shinar. And so it is with profound logic, and virtually inevitable, that Abraham is called from this rubble and promised a new hope in space. Indeed, as already seen, the threefold promise of land, fertility, and blessing given to Abraham effectively reverses the curses of the expulsion and so establish him as a new Adam. This point is structurally enforced by the fact that Abraham is born ten generations after Noah, who was himself born ten generations after Adam and proclaimed as the one who would "comfort us from our work and painful toil on the earth which YHWH has cursed" (Genesis 5:29; cf. 3:17).

Traces of the imagery of a sacred center slowly surface in the early national texts, although they may often lack the coherence, almost self-conscious deliberateness, of later materials. One may surmise that such vestigial representations are partially conditioned by the historiographic filter of these materials. Nevertheless, a distinct and singular exemplar of this image complex does surface in Genesis 28:10-22, in connection with the dream vision and promised blessing given to Jacob.

As if to counterpoint the hubris of the tower building on the plain of Shinar (Genesis 11:1-9), the image of a staged temple-tower, whose "head" also "reaches to heaven," emerges out of Jacob's dream-work and humbles him (v.12). He does'not seek to achieve a name at the nameless place to which he has come on his flight to Aram, but is rather overawed by the divine presence there and extols His name: "Surely YHWH is in this place," explains Jacob, "and I did not know it" (v.16). Nor does God collude with the pantheon in this text; but rather stands majestically above the divine beings whose "going up and coming down" the tower stairway provides the symbolic link between earth and heaven, and dramatizes the spiritual ascension inherent in the dream vision. From atop this tower stairway promise and hope—not doom and dispersal—now unfold (vv.13-15). So as to commemorate and concretize this moment, Jacob, upon awakening, externalizes his dream imagery and erects a pillar whose "head" he anoints with oil: For indeed this place was for him a sacred center, a "cosmic mountain" linking heaven and earth (v.18). It was, as he says, a Beth-el, a "house of God" and a "gateway to heaven" (v.17). And should he return from his journey in safety, Jacob also vows to recommemorate this pillar and transform it into a "House of Elohim" (vv.20-22).

The next clear instance of sacred center imagery strikingly recurs outside the promised land, at the advent of the fulfillment of the patriarchal promises. As such it mediates between type and antitype, between settlement in Canaan and slavery in Egypt. Thus when Israel is in Egypt, God commissions His servant Moses to announce the Redemption. The event occurs at the *sneh*-bush (Exodus 3:2), by the "mountain of God" (v.1). This place, on which Moses stands, is called *'admat qodesh*, "sacred space." As we have seen, Exodus

1-4 foreshadows Exodus 5-19, so that the *sneh* event with Moses (Exodus 3) anticipates the revelation to all Israel at *Sinai* (Exodus 19), which also burns and is comparably called a "mountain of God" (Exodus 24:13).

Thus the redemption from Egypt is announced, and the covenant consummated, at a cosmic mountain. And it is, moreover, at just this place, that Moses receives a divine blueprint of the earthly shrine he is to build (Exodus 25:9,40; 26:30; 27:8). What is meant, however mutedly expressed, is that the earthly shrine will be in the image of the heavenly. Indeed, as frequently reflected in the Bible (e.g., Isaiah 6; Ezekiel 1; 10; 40), the heavenly abode of God is experienced as directly above the earthly. This notion had wide currency in other parts of the ancient Near East as well, where the earthly temple was considered to be a replica of the cosmos itself and directly below the divine abode.[6]

As the throne of divine glory descending to earth, the ark stood in the religious center of the Tabernacle complex—not far from the candelabrum, whose design was heir to an ancient iconographic tradition associated with representations of the Tree of Life. Concentric spheres of holiness encompassed this ark in zones materially marked by the degrees of precious stones and woods used to build or ornament the various shrinal appurtenances. And when the ark traveled in the desert, so priestly tradition reports, the tribal encampment further encircled the ark in symmetrical orders (Numbers 2:1-31, esp. v.17). Truly the One of Sinai, and symbolically even Sinai itself, were transported with this ark which served as the mobile center of holiness as Israel made its way from Sinai to Canaan. For may one not observe incipient symbolism in the fact that the pillars of fire and smoke which protected Israel at the Exodus (Exodus 13:21), and which accompanied the awesome theophany of Sinai (Exodus 19:16,19), were redeployed around the entourage in its desert wanderings (e.g., Exodus 40:34-38)? In such a symbolic way was the sacred center of Sinai protected and relocated to the land called by God: "the mountain of My inheritance" (Exodus 15:17). It nevertheless remained for future singers of psalms to describe the transfer of Sinai to Canaan in more explicit terms.

With the monarchic period the "Eden" motif appears with more insistence and variety. The Davidic court theologians exalted Jerusalem, figuratively, as a new Sinai. They portrayed it in the imagery of Eden: as the mountain of God, as the locus of fructifying waters, as the point around which the sacred life of the community revolved.

Two psalms in particular, 68 and 78, reflect this transfer of Sinai imagery to Zion-Jerusalem. In Psalm 68:16–18, a competition is portrayed between "mountains of God" which express jealousy that Zion has been chosen to be the seat of YHWH's presence.

> Mount Bashan is a mountain of God:
>   Ridge-backed is Mount Bashan.
>
> Why do you contend, you ridge-backed mountains,
>   With the mountain which Elohim has desired for His abode?
> May YHWH dwell there forever!
>
> The chariots of Elohim are myriads,
>   thousands and thousands;
> The Lord has come from Sinai in holiness.*

God has come to Jerusalem from Sinai; Jerusalem has become the center to which gifts are brought from the world over (Psalm 68:30–33). "You are awesome, Elohim, from your shrine," says the psalmist. "Let Elohim be blessed!" (v.36).

The choice of Mount Zion as the seat of divine dwelling is more precisely specified in Psalm 78. After a succession of traditions and memories of divine acts is described, including the destruction of the Shilo shrine (v.60) and the exile of the north ("So He despised the tent of Joseph, and rejected the staff of Ephraim"; v.67), we read:

> Then He chose the staff of Judah,
>   Mount Zion which He loved;
> He built His shrine like the heights,
>   And fixed it firm like earth for all time.
>
> He chose David His servant,
>   And took him from the sheep-folds.
> He brought him from behind the ewes,
>   to shepherd [instead] His nation Jacob,
>   And over Israel His inheritance.
> And he shepherded them by his pure heart,
>   And led them by the wisdom of his deeds. (vv.68–72)

This closing strophe of the psalm, exalting the kingship of David and the new choice of Zion as the mountain of God's dwelling, is the climactic point of the many events described in this liturgy. It finds its prophetic correlate in the well-known

---

*Reading *b' msyny* ("come from Sinai") for Massoretic *bm syny*, with many scholars.

eschatological oracle of Isaiah of Jerusalem (eighth century B.C.E.):

> And it will be in future times that the mountain of the Temple of YHWH will be set on the summit of all mountains. It will rise above all hills and all peoples will flow to it. And many nations will go and say: "Come, let us go up to the Mountain of YHWH, to the Temple of the God of Jacob, that He may instruct us in His ways, so that we may follow in His paths." Surely instruction [Torah] will come forth from Zion, and the word of YHWH from Jerusalem. (2:2-3)

Zion is here forecast as the future center of teachings for all mankind. Like Sinai of old, Zion is a "mountain of YHWH" from which Torah will be revealed—only now to a reborn and universal world.

Several other psalms deepen the foregoing image of Jerusalem as a sacred center. Formed of vestiges and echoes of ancient mythographic imagery, they glorify Jerusalem as a world center and historical Eden, a "city of God" (Psalms 87:3), a divine dwelling from whose center flow "rejoicing" waters (Psalms 46:5; cf. 48:2-4, 12-14). It sits on the "mountain of YHWH" set over the cosmic deep (Psalms 48:3). Here, too, as Isaiah states (28:16), is the "foundation stone" of origins, an ancient symbol often found with images of sacred geography:[7]

> Therefore, thus says the Lord, YHWH:
> Behold I lay a stone in Zion,
> A tried stone, a costly cornerstone of
> firm foundation.

Elsewhere, as well, Isaiah calls Jerusalem "Ariel" (29:1), a term which means "mountain of God."[8] According to later biblical and ancient rabbinic tradition, Jerusalem's Temple was also the entrance point to the netherworld.[9] In and through Jerusalem, then, the upper heavens and the lower depths are joined.

The woe and dislocation of the exile were deeply felt; the destruction of Jerusalem and its Temple was mourned in Judea and Babylon. But once hopes of restoration began to surface in the prophecies of the postexilic prophets, visions of spatial renewal, shaped by the myth of an edenic center, found expression. The "Eden" motif now emerged with singular force and clarity. References to and expansions of the biblical symbolism of sacred geography become significantly abundant in the postexilic period.

Ezekiel, in his later eschatological oracles, envisions that the repurified land will be, for the returning exiles, a veritable "garden of Eden":

> Thus says the Lord, YHWH:
> When I shall purify you from your iniquities, I shall [also] restore the cities, and the ruins will be rebuilt. The desolate earth will be tilled, and will no longer be a desolation before every wayfarer. And they will remark: "This land, which was a desolation, has become like the garden of Eden; and the ruined, desolate, and rubbled cities have become fortified and inhabited." (36:33-55)

Isaiah of the Exile also centered his hopes on this spatial image when he encouraged the exiles to return (51:1-3):

> Listen to me, chasers of justice,
>   Seekers of YHWH.
> Look to the rock whence you were hewn,
>   And to the pit from which you were quarried.
> Look to Abraham your father,
>   And Sarah your genetrix.
> For when I called him he was [but] one,
>   Then I blessed him and made him many.
>
> Surely YHWH has pitied Zion,
>   had pity for her hovels.
> He has made her wilderness like Eden,
>   And her desert like the Garden of YHWH.
> Joy and mirth is to be found therein,
>   Thanksgiving and the plaint of music.

The return projected here is not described as a new Exodus, but as a repetition of Abraham's journey and settlement at the beginning of national history. As Abraham had reversed the doom and decay of religious life "east of Eden," so the entire people are now called upon to remember their origins and the blessings of the past and to return to the land of their forefathers, thus reversing the despair and slackened spirits of years in exile.

Restored from her ruins, Jerusalem will thus be like Eden, like a garden of the Lord. In it the primordial dream of simple natural harmony, a dream so massively shattered by the eviction from Paradise, will again be a waking reality:

> The wolf and lamb will graze *(yir'u)* together,
> And the lion will eat straw like cattle...

They shall neither hurt *(yare'u)* nor destroy
On all My holy mountain (Isaiah 65:24-25)

One recalls this vision from its first occurrence in Isaiah 11:6–9, where the hope of a transformation in nature is even extended to a new human playfulness with the deadly creatures of the earth. In its renewed expression here, the hope of exilic restoration to an edenic Zion is remarkably coupled with a projected reversal of the ancient curses of Genesis 3:16-19. The inhabitants of the new Jerusalem "will not toil in vain or give birth to misfortune; for they are [to be] the blessed progeny of YHWH, they and their offspring after them" (Isaiah 65:23). And the city itself, once proclaimed the matrix of all her far-flung people (Psalm 87:4-5), will again suckle her inhabitants and envigor them with new life and joy (Isaiah 66:11).

The images of Eden in Ezekiel and Isaiah become even more concrete and elaborate as they embroider visions of the new Temple. Ezekiel, a priest, knew intimately the harmony and order of the Temple. His mystical visions occur there (chaps. 1, 10); and, like a new Moses, he sees the blueprint of the rebuilt Temple of the future in a heavenly vision (chaps. 40–42). It is for this reason, without doubt, that the cultic abominations in Jerusalem cause him so much shame and anger (chaps. 8–11) and, further, that his vision of restoration takes the shape of a New Temple.

It is certainly striking in this context that Ezekiel, who participated in the Babylonian exile (after 597 B.C.E.), describes the base platform of the altar of his envisioned Temple as *heq ha'aretz,* "bosom of the earth," and its summit, crowned by four horns, as *har'el,* "mountain of God." For not only does *har'el* most likely reflect a popular etymology of the Akkadian word *arallu,* meaning "mountain of the gods" and "underworld,"[10] but *heq ha'aretz* is the precise Hebrew equivalent of the term used in contemporary Babylonian inscriptions to denote the base of the temple-tower or ziggurat.[11] Thus, through these two terms, Ezekiel utilizes ancient temple-tower/mountain symbolism to convey the axial significance of the altar as the sacred center of the Temple itself.

At the conclusion of his vision of the New Temple, Ezekiel's allusion to the altar as an *axis mundi,* a veritable world center for Judea and Jerusalem, is symbolically enhanced by the images of Eden (47:1-12):

> And he brought me to the door of the Temple; and, behold, waters were flowing eastward from under the threshold of the Temple . . . and the waters came down from under . . . on the south of the altar. And he took me out to the northern gate; . . . and, behold, waters poured from the right corner . . . then he said to me: "These waters flow out to the eastern territory and will course to the Aravah; and when they come to the sea, the sea of polluted waters, the waters shall be healed. And it will be that every living thing that swarms will be sustained whithersoever the rivers shall come; and there shall be a great multitude of fish. . . . And by the river will arise, on both banks, every type of tree for food. Its leaves will not wither nor will its fruit cease, but will ripen monthly—for its waters come out from the Shrine. Thus its fruit will be edible and its leaf will be for healing."

The new Temple, on a mountain, is an Eden: waters of sustenance and life flow from the threshold and altar of the shrine, just as pictured in numerous ancient iconographies and in postbiblical literature.[12] These waters, flowing from a sacred, restorative center, abound with fish and fertilize the life-giving and healing trees along its banks. The rich power of this motif is now fully evident. It arises from and taps the most primal of yearnings: a harmonious life on earth, with the grace of God.

Ezekiel's eschatological vision of a new, historical Eden comes to firm expression in a late oracle attributed to the prophet Zechariah. A time is yet coming, the prophet says, when waters of life will spread from Jerusalem to all the earth. The tensions of space will give way to order and harmony; anxiety will yield to trust and security. This unity of space is crystallized by the unity of YHWH's rule over the entire earth, when He will be One and His name One (14:8–11):

> And it will be on that day: living waters will come out of Jerusalem, half going to the eastern sea and half towards the western. So it will be in both summer and winter. And YHWH will be King over all the earth; on that day YHWH will be One and His name One. . . . And all shall dwell therein; and there shall be no more extermination; and Jerusalem will dwell in safety.

Similarly, the late prophet Joel, no stranger to oracles of wrath, contrasts visions of disorder with visions of hope. The land, once likened to the garden of Eden but now in ruins (2:3), will, on a future day of divine restoration, be restored to its ancient glory. His vision is saturated with edenic images which accentuate the role of the Temple in a mythograph of renewed harmony and blessing:

And it will be on that day:
Mountains will drip sweet liquid
  And the hills shall flow with milk;
All the brooks of Judea will flow with water,
  And a fountain shall burst out from the
Temple of YHWH and water the Valley of Shittim.

Judea will be inhabited for ever,
  And Jerusalem from generation to generation.
And I will forgive those not yet pardoned,
  For YHWH will dwell in Zion. (4:18, 20–21)

Once again the primordial imagery of Eden surfaces to express man's deepest longings for harmony. Its recurrence traces a trajectory from prehistory to its earthly transfigurations; from the primal world center to its several relocations along the fractured face of history. Lodged deep in the shadows of archetypal memory, and seemingly resistant to external experience, the imagery of Eden expresses a resilient human trust in the beneficence of the earth. Aided by this memory-turned-hope, the successive separations from Eden marked in the Bible are vigorously and remarkably transformed into new occasions for historical renewal.

Mankind was evicted bodily from Eden; but the latter's mysterious force retains a hold on its imagination, eliciting the longings of a mortal mankind condemned to the terrors, dislocations, and finality of historical existence.[13] But as such projections of a new Eden are limited by their intended locus within history, it remained for another word of God to envision an end to the travail of time itself. Referring to a future celebration at a sacred center, Isaiah says:

Upon this mountain YHWH of Hosts will prepare
A rich banquet for all the nations:
A banquet of well-kept wine and rich food,
A banquet of well-kept wine strained of its lees.

Upon this mountain He will swallow up the veil
  Which shrouds mankind, the pall cast on all;

He will swallow up death forever; indeed, the Lord YHWH
  Will wipe the tears from off each face,
And remove his people's reproach from the earth.

Surely! YHWH has spoken. (25:6–8)

10. The "Exodus" Motif / The Paradigm of Historical Renewal

The "exodus" motif has more internal coherence than the "Eden" motif since many of its expressions refer to the first exodus, and since it recurs in texts of each generation. In contrast to an image of renewal in space, the "exodus" motif emphasizes the temporal-historical paradigm in whose image all future restorations of the nation are to be manifest. A concord between the first and succeeding redemptions is the issue, for each generation looked to the first exodus as the archetypal expression of its own future hope.

The narrative of the exodus from Egypt in Exodus 1-15, as noted earlier, depicted this historical event as the consummate expression of divine power and national redemption. The interweaving of a broad diversity of recollections of this event into a coherent and expanded saga of cumulative force resulted in a *mythos* of the origins of Israelite religious consciousness and nationhood. Accordingly, the exodus tradition was used, from the first, as a paradigmatic teaching for present and future generations. Its incorporation into the texts of national origin served as a permanent record of the beneficent acts of God for Israel.

Throughout the opening chapters of the Book of Deuteronomy, for example, various sermons refer to the exodus as the primary historical event of national origin. It was the antecedent to the fulfillment of the promise to the patriarchs: the entrance into the land of Canaan. Accordingly, the Lord who redeemed Israel from Egypt is acknowledged in these sermons as the very Land-Lord of Canaan, and His covenantal stipulations are considered the living bond between Himself and the people about to settle there (cf. 7:12-26; 8:1-18; 11:1-9). The recollection of the exodus traditions often takes the didactic form of question and answers, as in Deuteronomy 6:20-25, a text explored in an earlier chapter; and its remembrance was also kept alive through historical sermons (e.g., Joshua 24; Judges 2:11ff.; 1 Samuel 12:6ff.), individual prayers (e.g., Jeremiah 32:16ff.; Daniel 9:4ff.), and national liturgies (e.g., Psalms 78 and 105). In all these ways the exodus became a *mythos*: a life teaching through which an "objective past" recurrently gave way to a subjectivized event of the present.

A more penetrating means of preserving the exodus event in national consciousness was its reuse as a literary motif.[1] As such, it became a lens of historical perception and anticipation for succeeding generations.

The exodus from Egyptian bondage was bound to the conquest of the promised land of Canaan. Indeed, the divine oracle to Abraham in Genesis 15:13–16 ties the inheritance of the land to a future restoration from a land of bondage. Abraham's trust (stem: *'amen*) in God's promise (15:6) became the inheritance of his descendants both before (4:28–31) and after the exodus (14:31). Such a wondrous event as the conquest could not be adequately portrayed by descriptive reportage alone, or even by such images as wailing trumpets and falling walls, secret plots and scarlet ribbons, magic circles, adroit military ploys, and such other features as appear in Joshua 2–7. For those who remembered the conquest as an event of their own lives, and for those historian-theologians who reflected on it as an event in the life of the people, it appeared that history was repeating itself. And so reflective historiography seized upon the deepest and most indelible cultural memory of redemption: the exodus from Egypt. The conquest of Canaan and the crossing of the Jordan River were recollected, then, as a reenactment of this formative and paradigmatic event. Before the battle at Jericho, Joshua tells the people to sanctify themselves, "for tomorrow YHWH will do wonders in your midst" (Joshua 3:5).

> Then YHWH said to Joshua: "I will exalt you this day in the eyes of all Israel, that they may know that I will be with you just as I was with Moses." (v.7)

A typological link between Moses and Joshua is hereby anticipated. The text continues in vv.9–17 with the following charge by Joshua to the priests who stand with the ark on the banks of the Jordan, before its crossing:

> "Come forward and hear the words of YHWH your God. . . . By the following you will know that the living God is in your midst, and that He will surely disinherit the Canaanite, the Hittite, the Hivite, the Perizzite, the Girgashite, the Amorite and the Jebusite. . . . It shall happen that when the soles of the feet of the priests who bear the ark of YHWH, Lord of all the earth, touch the waters of the Jordan, the Jordan waters will be split—these are the waters that flow down from above—and stand as a wall."

> And it happened that the people took up their tents to cross the Jordan; and the priests, who bore the ark of the covenant, went before the people. And when...the feet of the priests who were bearing the ark were dipped into the water's edge—for the Jordan was filled to its banks during the harvest season—that the waters that flowed down from above stood and arose as a wall...and the priests who bore the ark of the covenant of YHWH stood firmly on dry ground in the midst of the Jordan...until the entire nation completed the crossing of the Jordan.

One cannot fail to hear in this passage the echoes of the crossing of the sea after the exodus from Egypt: the Israelites crossed the Jordan dry-shod during the springtime, at harvest season, when the torrents of water piled up around them like a wall. This fusing of two separate events of redemption in the soul of ancient Israel achieved a poetic-liturgical expression:

> The [Reed] Sea looked and fled,
> The Jordan turned tail in fright (Psalm 114:3).

The preceding interpretation of the link between the exodus and the conquest is buttressed by the introductory statement that Joshua would be exalted before Israel, "just as" Moses, his predecessor, was (3:7). The phraseology of this text recapitulates the language of the earlier divine commission to Joshua in 1:5 ("as I was with Moses I shall be with you"), and anticipates the phraseology which follows the crossing of the Jordan:

> On that day YHWH exalted Joshua in the eyes of all Israel; and they feared him *just as* they feared Moses all the days of his life. (4:14)

Further links between the conquest and exodus events appear after the crossing:

> And it was when the priests, who were bearing the ark of YHWH came up from the Jordan, [and] as soon as the soles of the priests touched dry ground, the waters of the Jordan returned to their place and flowed over its banks as previously.
> So the people went up from the Jordan on the tenth day of the first month, and camped at Gilgal on the eastern border of Jericho. And Joshua set up those twelve stones which they took out of the Jordan, saying as follows to the people of Israel: "When your children shall ask their fathers in the future, saying: 'What are these stones?' you shall inform your children, saying: 'Israel crossed this Jordan on dry land. For YHWH your God dried up the waters of the Jordan from before you until you crossed; just as YHWH your God did at the Reed Sea, which he dried up before us

> until we had crossed: that all the nations of the earth might know
> that the arm of YHWH is mighty; that you might fear YHWH
> your God for ever.'" (4:18-24)

Not only is the link between Moses and Joshua explicitly
established in this passage, insofar as God dried up waters for
both, but a significant temporal link between the exodus and
conquest is established as well. The text states that the
Israelites arrived at the site of Gilgal on the tenth day of the
first month; and on the fourteenth

> they performed the paschal offering on the plains of Jericho. And
> they ate of the produce of the land on the morrow of the paschal
> meal—unleavened cakes and parched corn—even on that day.
> (5:10-11)

Significantly, then, the Israelites are depicted as celebrating
their entrance into the land of Canaan, in the first month, with
the cake ritual and paschal offering of the Passover. The
homology with the first Passover, also celebrated on the eve of
the fourteenth day of the first month, could not be more precise
or pointed. With the entrance into the land the food of
wandering (the manna) is put aside and the bread of redemption (the unleavened cakes) is eaten again (v.12).

A final link between the exodus and the conquest in Joshua
3-5 deserves mention. Immediately after the ceremony at
Gilgal and before the invasion of Jericho, a messenger of
YHWH, his sword unsheathed, addresses Joshua: "Take your
sandals from off your feet, for the place upon which you are
standing is sacred" (v.15). On the brink of battle, about to
complete the preexodus promises of God to the patriarchs,
Joshua is again addressed as a new Moses.

This historiographical fusion of the exodus and conquest
found an early poetic-liturgical realization in Exodus 15. Two
parts are discernible in this composition: Part 1, vv.1-11, deals
with the Pharoah, the Egyptian enemy, the "walling up" of the
waters, and the drowning of the Egyptians in the sea; Part 2,
vv.12-18, deals with the might of God against the original,
native population of Philistia, Edom, Moab, and Canaan, their
rout and defeat and the Israelites' entrance into the land.
While this second part has been connected with the preceding
one through verbal and thematic links (e.g., the right hand of
God, vv. 6 and 12; the divine *'oz*, "power," vv. 2 and 13; the
walling up of water, vv. 4 and 13; and the fall of the enemies
like a "stone," vv. 5 and 16) it clearly deals with a different

historical circumstance: the conquest.[2] And yet it is precisely these rhetorical links between the parts that disclose the layering of Israel's historical consciousness, a layering which fit new events to the archetypal armature of its formative experiences. Deeply constitutive of its reflective imagination, this process predisposed Israel's projective imagination as well.

An early expression of the exodus motif in the context of anticipation and restoration occurs in the Book of Hosea (eighth century B.C.E.). In the opening chapter, God commanded the prophet to take a whore to wife so as to simulate the infidelity which Israel, as bride, had shown to Him through her constant attraction to Ba'al and the gods of Canaan (2:7). Towards the end of the criticism, mixed with threats of punishment and destruction, words of hope are heard. God announces that He Himself will effectuate a change and renewal:

> Therefore, behold, I will entice her and lead her out to the steppe, and woo her. And I will give her her vineyards from there, and [transform] the Emeq of Achor [valley of sorrow] to Petah Tiqvah [gate of hope]. And she shall be refreshed as in the time of her youth, when she came up from the land of Egypt. (2:16-17)

Both the exodus and conquest motifs are subtly intertwined in this oracle of hope. God promises to reverse the misadventure of the first conquest by enticing Israel back into the desert, recovenant her to Himself (vv.18ff.), and restore her once again to the land. At that time the valley of sorrow *(Achor)*, the point of reentry, will become the "gate of hope," i.e., that very place where Israel first sinned upon entering the land, through the ritual violation of Achan (Joshua 7:1)—called *Achor* in 1 Chronicles 2:7—will become the portal to a new life. The people "shall be refreshed as in the time of her youth, when she came up from the land of Egypt." History serves here as a prism of hope; the future will reclaim a stained past.

The potential of the exodus event to provide hope is revealed in several oracles from the end of the eighth century. Mighty Assyria then menaced the ancient Near East, hovering over the nations. The prophet Micah encourages the national aspirations of Israel, foretelling a time when Israel will arise from the ruins of the Assyrian empire. His colloquy with God dramatizes this hope:

Tend Your people, the flock of Your inheritance,
  with Your staff;
Let those that dwell alone, like stubble in a field,
  pasture in Bashan and Gilead, as they used to.
"I will surely show him wonders
  as when you came up from Egypt." (7:14-15)

In this passage, the prophet admonishes God, who responds: the future redemption will be a renewal of past wonders. The ·reference to exodus here serves to articulate the felt inner unity of Israel's history with God. The pain of historical pressures would dissipate. Assurance lay in references to times past.

Micah's contemporary, Isaiah, also urged confidence in the Holy One of Israel, though his trust was more passive. Amid his prophecies for the holy remnant and its hope of a restoration of Zion under a Davidic King of justice and right, Isaiah delivers the following oracle:

And it will be on that day;
The Lord will set His hand again, a second time,
  to recover the remnant of His people,
Which will remain from Assyria, Egypt, Pathros and Ethiopia,
  from Elam, Shinar, Hamath, and the Aegean isles.
And He will set a sign for the nations,
  and gather the dispersed of Israel;
He will assemble the scattered of Judah,
  from the four corners of the earth.
Then will the envy of Ephraim depart,
  and the troubles of Judah be sundered.
Ephraim will no longer envy Judah,
  and Judah will no longer trouble Ephraim.
They will fly westward to the Philistine coast,
  and together despoil the people of the east;
They will put forth their hand against Edom and Moab,
  and the people of Ammon will obey them.
Then will YHWH destroy the delta of the sea of Egypt,
  and raise His hand against the Nile;
By the blast of His wind he will cleave the Sea,*
  will smite it into seven streams,
  and lead people through dry-shod.
There will be a paved way for the remnant of His people,
  which will remain, from Assyria,

---

*Ibn Ezra suggest that the stems *hrm,* "destroy," and *nkh,* "smite," refer to the splitting of the Sea at the Exodus. I suggest that the impossible *ba'yam* be read *baqa' yam,* "cleave the Sea." This correction, which assumes that the *q* was accidentally dropped, produces a phrase like Exodus 14:21 and Psalms 78:13.

> Even as it was for Israel
>> when it came up from the land of Egypt. (11:11-16)

The return of the remnant of Israel from exile would be a second exodus. "The Lord will set His hand…*a second time* to recover the remnant of His people." Nation after nation is mentioned: Assyria, Egypt, Pathros, Ethiopia, Elam, Shinar, Hamath, and the Aegean isles. The returnees will come "from the four corners of the earth." Israel would soon be redeemed from its exile and servitude in Assyria, "as it was…when it came up from the land of Egypt." God will smite the Nile and cleave the Sea; He will hew it into seven streams and lead the victors through dry-shod.

The mighty blasts of wind which split the sea recall the first exodus: Just as the God of Israel won a victory over the sea *(yam)* during the occasion of Israel's first redemption (Exodus 14:21), so now, at this second exodus, He will again smite the sea *(yam)* and "cleave" it asunder (cf. Psalm 78:13). Such imagery preserves vestigial traces of battles with sea monsters known to ancient Near Eastern cosmogonies. In the Bible, such imagery is mostly restricted to creation texts (e.g., Psalms 74:12-14; 89:11; 104:6f.). Their reuse in connection with the exodus (old and new) deepens its evocative force as an event of origins.[3] In fact, this appropriation of creation imagery extends to the activities of Moses. Just as he, with a magical staff, cleaved the sea *(yam)* in Exodus 14:16, so Ba'al, in Canaanite literature, destroyed his archenemy *Yam* (Sea), the "seven-headed monster," with his magical staff.[4] In a comparable way, Marduk, in *Enuma elish*, the Babylonian epic of creation, killed and cleaved the sea monster Tiamat with his lance and mighty blasts of the winds.

This ancient combat imagery can be detected in Exodus 15 as well. YHWH is referred to as a warrior (v.3) whose arm smashes the enemy (v.6); and whose mighty wind splits the watery deeps *(tehomot;* cf. *ti'amat)*, causing them to congeal and pile up like a wall (v.8). This in itself is striking. But what is of added interest is the recurrence in this hymn of the common mythological structure discussed in the opening chapter, in which a temple is erected for the enthronement of the god who vanquishes the forces of chaos. Despite its historical emphasis, Exodus 15 is clearly structured around this ancient literary model.[5] For, after describing the victories of YHWH, the song refers to

The place You have established for Your dwelling, O YHWH, The
shrine, O Lord, which Your own hands have built. (v.17)

and concludes with an assertion and evocation of divine
kingship: "May YHWH reign forever and ever" (v.18).[6]
    The muted mythological imagery of warriors, winds, and
wands in Exodus 14-15 comes fully to the fore in Isaiah 11:11-
16. Such imagery is undoubtedly rooted in popular expressions
and recollections of the ancient exodus. Historical redemption
is, so to speak, a renewal of national origins, and uses the
mythography of creation for dramatic emphasis.

    In another example of the exodus motif, traditionally
accredited to Isaiah, a series of eschatological oracles are
announced to Egypt (19:19-25). Its transformation of early
traditions is ironic and audacious:

> On that day:
> There will be an altar to YHWH in the midst of Egypt,
>   and a stela to YHWH near its border.
> And it will be a sign and witness to YHWH of hosts in
>   Egypt, that when they cry out to YHWH because
>   of their oppressors He will send a savior and
>   leader who will rescue them.
> Thus YHWH will be known to Egypt; and Egypt will know
>   YHWH on that day; and they will worship with
>   meat and meal, will make vows to YHWH and repay [them].
> Then will YHWH smite Egypt a fearful smiting,
>   that they return to YHWH; and he will assuage
>   and heal them.
>
> On that day:
> There will be a highway from Egypt to Assyria;
>   Assyria will come to Egypt and Egypt to Assyria;
>   and Egypt will serve Assyria.
>
> On that day:
> Israel will form the third part with Egypt and Assyria;
>   a blessing in the midst of the earth—
> Which YHWH of hosts has blessed, saying:
>
>> "Blessed be Egypt, My people,
>> and Assyria, My handiwork,
>> and Israel, My inheritance."

    Isaiah's capacity to transpose exodus traditions can be most
suggestively seen when the foregoing passage is juxtaposed to

the language of the exodus cycle, particularly Exodus 3:7-9 and 8:16-24. In these latter passages YHWH sees the torment of "my people" *('ammi)*; hears their cry *(tza'aqatam)*; sees the Egyptians oppressing *(lohatzim)* them; and sends (stem: *shalah)* Moses as a deliverer to bring them out. When He sends a sign *('ot)* that the Egyptians might know (stem: *yada')* His power, Pharaoh temporarily relents to let the Israelites sacrifice (stem: *zabah)* to YHWH in Egypt—but Moses refuses. The Israelites would worship YHWH only outside Egypt. Pharaoh also begs Moses to pray (stem: *'atar)* for him. Punishment for Pharaoh's noncompliance with Moses' demands is that YHWH will plague the Egyptians. (The stem: *nagaf,* meaning "to plague," is also found in Exodus 7:27; 12:23; and Joshua 24:5.)

By means of an exegetical-terminological counterpoint, Isaiah 19:19-25 touches on all the foregoing features of the exodus tradition and radically transforms them. Now the Egyptians have oppressors *(lohatzim)* and cry *(yitz'aqu)* to YHWH; and now an altar to YHWH, built in Egypt, will be a sign *('ot)* that He will send (stem: *shalah)* them a deliverer. Through these acts of deliverance YHWH will be known (stem: *yada')* to the Egyptians, and they will sacrifice (stem: *zabah)* to Him. YHWH will plague *(nagaf)* the Egyptians; but in the end He will respond to their prayers (stem: *'atar)*.

Taken altogether, a striking inversion and metamorphosis of the exodus motif is produced in Isaiah 9:19-25. Egypt will, in the future, turn to the God of Israel who will redeem them through a savior. No longer is the exodus the private tradition of Israel alone: it becomes the symbolic form through which a messianic moment is envisaged. Egypt, the first oppressor of Israel, will one day have its share in an "exodus"-type event. To be sure, Amos had earlier emphasized that Israel's God was not the historical redeemer of Israel alone: "Are you not like Ethiopians to Me, O Israel, oracle of YHWH; for did I not bring the Israelites up from Egypt, the Philistines from Caphtor, and the Arameans from Qir?" (9:7). For Amos, Israel's claim to uniqueness lay in the covenant (3:1-2)—and this it had forsaken.

But Amos does not go as far as Isaiah. With his daring transformation—not just relativization—of the national tradition, Isaiah pushed the language of cultural memory to the limit of its innermost possibilities. This is acutely felt in 19:25, where Egypt is called "My people" *('ammi)*. In fact, such a transfer of a designation used pointedly of Israel (e.g., Exodus

3:10) weighed heavily on ancient Jewish translators. Unable to tolerate such a theological paradox, the Septuagint and Targum traditions renationalized the text and substituted Israel for Egypt.

The shaping power of the exodus motif continued into succeeding generations. Looking to a future time of national unity, when the exiles of the north would be rejoined to their people, Jeremiah, speaking in the seventh century, formulates this hope as a new exodus:

> Therefore, behold days are coming—oracle of YHWH—when no one will say: "By the life of YHWH who brought the people of Israel up from the land Egypt," but [rather]: "By the life of YHWH who brought the people of Israel up from the land of the north, and from all lands whithersoever He had dispersed them." And I will restore them to their land which I gave to their fathers. (16:14-15)

This formulation, phrased as a radically new teaching ("behold days are coming...when no one will say...but [rather]"), is similar to other Jeremian texts which anticipate a religious change in the future (cf. 3:16; 7:22f.; and 31:28f.,33; where the phrase "in future days...no longer...but" recurs). But it also reveals the significance of the exodus in the national imagination of Israel in a pointed way. For it would appear that in Jeremiah's day, when one swore by the power of the God of Israel, he did so not only "by the life of YHWH," but especially by His historical attribute: He "who brought the people of Israel up from Egypt." This last phrase is not so much a theological epithet (like "the Holy One of Israel," or "the God of all spirits and life," or "Who dwells upon the cherubim") as a historical characterization of divine power similar to phrases like "Who saves Israel" in 1 Samuel 14:39, or "Who delivered me from all trouble" in 2 Samuel 4:9 and 1 Kings 1:29.

Thus the force of YHWH as a guarantor of an oath is, in Jeremiah 16:14-15, directly related to remembrance of His power at the exodus. But, says the oracle, days are coming when the designation will change. For YHWH will soon bring the exiled Israelites back from their dispersion in the north. Their return to the ancestral land will be a new exodus. On that day, and ever again in remembrance of it, people will swear "by the life of YHWH who brought the people of Israel up from the land of the north, and from all the lands whithersoever He had dispersed them." This hope for a national ingathering, reflected in Isaiah 11:11-6, is repeated in Jeremiah 23:7-8.

With the successive exiles of the Judeans in the sixth century (597 and 587/6), the exodus motif shifts its focus to those in the Babylonian exile. Ezekiel (Jeremiah's contemporary), who prophesied in Babylonia, is the first to utilize the motif in this way.

In Ezekiel 20, during the seventh year of the exile of King Jehoiakin of Judea (ca. 590), some of those Babylonian exiles approached the prophet to seek an oracle from the Lord. Though the contents of their query is not revealed, A. Menes, and more recently M. Greenberg, have suggested that the request was for permission to establish cultic worship in Babylon.[7] Other suggestions have been made also; but what is significant for our present purposes is that Ezekiel, presumably reflecting an otherwise unknown tradition, presents a long diatribe against the idolatry and apostasy of the Israelites when yet in Egypt and later in the desert wanderings. Indeed, while yet in Egypt, they had succumbed to the pagan environment so that God thought to destroy them with an angry fury. It is against this backdrop that the oracle of a new exodus from Babylon, where the Israelites in their servitude are again succumbing to idolatry and apostasy, is to be understood:

> As I live—oracle of the Lord, YHWH—surely with a strong hand, and an outstretched arm, and with pouring fury, will I rule over you. And I will bring you out from the peoples, and gather you from the lands to which you were scattered, with a strong hand, and an outstretched arm and with pouring fury. And I will bring you to the steppe [desert] of the peoples and I will adjudicate with you, face to face. Just as I adjudicated with your ancestors in the wilderness [desert] of the land of Egypt so will I adjudicate with you—oracle of the Lord, YHWH. Then I will bring you into the bond of the covenant. And I will cleanse you of those who rebel and transgress against Me. I will take them out of the lands of their dwelling; but they will not enter the land of Israel. Then you will know that I am YHWH. (vv.33-38)

This expression of divine wrath distinctly contrasts the tradition that the original exodus was an act of grace in fulfillment of ancient promises to the patriarchs. Ezekiel may well have intended to make such an ironic comparison because the language of 20:5-10, and particularly 20:33-42, is precisely the language of God's speech to Moses in Exodus 6:6-8. The relationship between these texts can be fully appreciated by the following comparison of content:

Exodus 6:6-8		*Ezekus 20:33-42*
vehotze'tiy	"I will take [you] out"	*vehotze'tiy*
bizro'a netuyah	"with an outstretched arm"	*bizro'a netuyah*
ubishefatim	"and with judgments"	*venishpatti* "I will judge"
viyda'tem kiy 'ani YHWH	"that you may know that I am YHWH"	*viyda'tem kiy 'ani YHWH*
veheve'tiy	"and I will bring [you]"	*behavi'iy* "when I bring [you]"
'el ha'aretz	"to the land"	*'el admath Yisrael* "to the land of Israel"
'asher nasa'tiy 'et yadiy	"which I swore (lit., "raised my hand")"	*'asher nasa'tiy 'et yadiy*
latet 'otah	"to give it"	*latet 'otah*
leAvaraham, le Yitzhaq, u-le Ya-'aqov	"to Abraham, Isaac, and Jacob"	*la'avotekhem* "to your forefathers"

Because of the intentional reuse of Exodus 6:6-8, Ezekiel's oracle takes on a heightened effect. Its sarcasm and bitterness were undoubtedly not lost on his first audience.

In his later oracles, Ezekiel does—as seen in the preceding chapter—present visions of hope relating to the land and Temple. However, it was only with a later prophet, one who did not have the bitterness of a recent exile, that the proper tone of consolation was reached. That prophet was Isaiah of the exile (Isaiah 40-55). Through him God spoke oracles of encouragement to the people, urging them to return to Canaan: "Do not fear," it is repeatedly said, "I shall be with you." Through deliberate allusion to the commission language of Moses and other prophets (cf. Exodus 3:12; Jeremiah 1:8; Ezekiel 2:6), he recalls the people to their prophetic destiny. In this context of reinforcement and support, the people were able to hear the "new things" which God was about to perform for his people.

References to "new things" recur in prophecies of the later Isaiah of the exile and are contrasted to "former things."

Scholars have occasionally interpreted this polarity in terms of the liberating decree of Cyrus for release from exile. But there may, perhaps, be a more nuanced range to these terms. In 41:22 and 42:9 the "new things" apparently refer to the prophecies of hope which had accompanied the former (preexilic) oracles of doom. Since these latter did come to pass, Isaiah suggests, the prophecies of consolation would also be realized. The issue of "former" and "later" things seems, in these two texts, to relate to God's fulfillment of His historical promises. In 65:16-18, by contrast, the prophecy is that "former" earthly woes will be transformed only when the dawn of salvation breaks over a "new heaven and new earth." The renewal of life will be permanent (66:22).

The exodus event is also used as a "former thing"—to which the "new" salvation-restoration will correspond.[8] Isaiah 43:18 clearly refers to a new exodus in vv.16-21, as the following suggests:

> Thus says YHWH,
>> Who made a path in the sea,
>>> And a way through mighty waters;
>> Who led forth [to doom]* horse and chariot, hero and troop:
>>> They fell altogether, never to rise again;
>>> They were trampled, snuffed out like flax.
>
> Do not recall the former things,
>> Nor think e'er of olden times:
> Behold, I shall do a new thing, just see it bloom!
>> Don't you sense it yet?!
> I shall make a path in the sea,
>> And streams in the barren waste:
> Wild beasts will do Me honor:
>> The jackal and even the ostrich;
> For I shall fill the waste with water,
>> And the barren waste with streams—
>>> To give drink to My chosen people!
>
> The nation which I have created will yet recount
> My praise.

The above oracle pivots on v.18: "Do not recall the former things." Preceding this admonition, God is described as He who delivered Israel from Egypt and brought them through the sea. Concluding it is God's reference to "the nation which I

---

*Instead of this elliptical formulation, the New Jewish Publica. Society *Isaiah* (1972;p.126) translates "Who destroyed," noting that *"Hosi* is here equivalent to Aramaic *shesi."* Cf. Ezra 6:15.

have created" *('am zu yatzartiy)*, a pointed allusion to the designation of Israel in the postexodus Song of the Sea (Exodus 15) as "the nation which I have created/redeemed" *('am zu qaniytiy/ga'altiy*; vv.16,13). This rhetorical enclosure, descriptive of former things and olden times, sets off and stands in direct contrast to the new event to come—the deliverance from Babylonian servitude—presented in very similar language. In the past "YHWH...made a path in the sea"; in the future He "shall make a path in the sea." This direct allusion to the exodus made, the prophet properly packs his oracles with references to the desert sojourn, though deleting those which describe the ancient Egyptian horse and rider. The way through the desert between Babylon and Canaan with "drink" is, no doubt, an allusion to the old journey through the Sinai waste when the terrors of drought were miraculously quenched (cf. Exodus 17:1-7). Isaiah expands on this theme in 48:20-21, where the ancient wandering and sustenance themes of the Book of Exodus (see 17:3-6) are directly referred to:

> Get out of Babylon,
>   Flee the Chaldeans!
> With victory shouts proclaim this and make it known,
>   Broadcast it to the ends of the earth.
> Say: "YHWH has redeemed His servant Jacob;
>   Though He led them through the desert,
>   They never did thirst;
>   He caused water to flow from a rock,
>   He cleaved a rock and water streamed forth!"

The situation of divine sustenance in the desert is elsewhere referred to by Isaiah, together with the language of "leaving" (49:9-11). And, on occasion, the contrast between the first leaving and the new exodus takes on ironic tones. Thus in 52:11-12 the people are given exact instructions: "You will not leave in haste [*hepazon*], nor go in flight." This recalls the precise language of the paschal sacrifice and ritual in Exodus 12:11:

> "And this is how you shall eat it:
> your loins girded, your sandals on your
> feet and your staff in your hand;
> and you shall eat it in haste [*hepazon*]."

The new teaching of Isaiah juxtaposes the calm departure of the new exodus with the disquietude of the first.

Out of the dark despair of exile, and reflecting a sense of

enslavement and loss of hope, this prophet seizes upon images of redemption whereby Israel's ancient and mysterious God would be recognized. Nowhere is this more strongly felt than in 51:9–11, where the *creation, exodus,* and *new exodus* are fused:

> Arise! Arise! Put on strength, arm of YHWH;
> Arise as in days of old, far-flung generations.
> > Are You not the one who hewed Rahab, and pierced Tanin?
> > Are You not the one who shriveled Yam, and the waters of
> > > mighty Tehom?
> > Who made a way through Yam, for the redeemed to pass?
> O may the redeemed of YHWH return,
> May they come to Zion garlanded in joy;
> > O may happiness and joy drive them on,
> > may they rout anguish and woe!

This incantation-prayer integrates three time dimensions in one interlocking web: the divine power of creation, the remembered redemptive power of national origins, and the longed-for reconstitution in a future redemptive recreation. In the primal past it was the "arm of YHWH" which had destroyed Rahab and Tanin, Yam and Tehom: ancient sea monsters all; and it was this same "arm" which cleaved Yam (the Sea personified) at the time of the exodus. Taking hope in these ancient manifestations of divine power, Isaiah invokes this same "arm of YHWH" to "put on strength" for those yet in exile, and speedily restore them to Zion.

Such a juxtaposition of a primordial time of cosmic order and a future time when the chaos of historical disorder will be ended is common in the Bible. The past is usually portrayed in mythographic images which serve to dramatize the former struggle and the present expectation. Just as God, aforetimes, destroyed the enemies of cosmic order, so will He soon, even now, destroy the perpetrators of historical evil. Isaiah 27:1 is a case in point:

> On that day YHWH will requite
> > Leviathan, the scaley serpent,
> > And Leviathan, the twisted serpent,
> With His sharp, great, and mighty sword;
> And He will kill the serpent who is in the sea.

The preceding is not a new creation from a precreation chaos; it is, rather, a new event within history. Just as this imagery had formerly provided the means for dramatizing the divine power when faced by antagonistic forces, so now it gives concrete shape to the destruction of the forces of evil in history. The prayer in Habakkuk 3 also utilizes such imagery, known from ancient Canaan. The battle is drawn in that context with bold and graphic colors (vv.8–15). The forces and order of creation will again be manifest: for He who created the world is also the god of Israel's historical salvation.[9]

The recurrence of cosmogonic combat imagery in connection with historical redemption, or the projected end of historical disorder, discloses a profound inner-biblical dialectic between the mythicization of history and the historicization of myth. For to the extent that biblical historical descriptions are rhetorically transposed by the infusion of paradigmatic mythic structures, the result of which is the very transvaluation of the events so described, it is equally significant that the biblical reuse of cosmogonic combat imagery does not simply serve to describe primordial events, but primarily underpins those whose locus is historical existence. In a culture like ancient Israel's, cognizant of the theological imperatives of a once-for-all creation, world renewal would logically and necessarily be envisioned in terms of historical renewal. But the inverse proposition is equally valid; namely, that the historical representation of past and future in terms of cosmogonic paradigms discloses the deep biblical presentiment that all historical renewal is fundamentally a species of world renewal.

The fact of exile is such, however, that one easily loses contact with one's spiritual ground—a situation which affected the exiles of Judea and their confidence in God's power. Like the Israelites of ancient Egypt, they had trouble hearing the new words of hope because of "a stifled spirit" (Exodus 6:9). Amazed and offended, God refers to His past acts, and asks:

> Why have I come and there is no one,
>   called and there is no response?
> Is my arm too weak for redemption,
>   or am I totally without power to save?
> Surely by My roar I shrivel Yam,
>   and turn the rivers into a wasteland;
> Their fish stink for lack of water,
>   and die because of thirst.
> I cloak the heavens with darkness,
>   and make their covering a rag. (Isaiah 50:2–3)

In this compressed outburst of rage, God roars at the people and asks whether His "arm" is "too weak" or withered "to save"—an oblique but ironically comprehensible allusion to His "mighty arm" or destructive power during the exodus from Egypt (Exodus 14:31; cf. 15:6,12). This query gives way, in turn, to a depiction of YHWH's triumphant power over Yam, the Sea. But whether the language actually refers to the tradition of a primordial combat between YHWH and the sea monster (cf. Isaiah 51:9), to the splitting of the sea at the exodus (cf. Isaiah 51:10), or to a future battle in the image of the one or the other, cannot be determined. Not only are the allusions indeterminate, but the very depictions teeter on a vertiginous ambiguity. Thus while the verbs denoting divine actions have been translated above neutrally, in the present tense, it is to be noted that they are constructed with the prefix form. This form commonly expresses future and present-future actions in biblical Hebrew; but it also reflects a more archaic and less common perfect, or past tense (e.g., Exodus 15:1; Numbers 23:7; Psalms 93:3).

How, then, should one construe the verbs? Does God speak of His past deeds (e.g., "I shriveled Yam"); of His present activity or capacity ("by My roar I shrivel Yam"); or of His future actions ("I will shrivel Yam")?[10] Determination of this matter has decisive bearing on the rhetorical thrust and theological implications of the passage. If the verbs denote past or present actions, they would presumably both be statements of proof made in response to the opening rhetorical question about His power; the difference between the two being that in the one case God lists His formal accomplishments, whereas in the other He attests to a present capacity or activity. One might even detect in this differentiation a shift from a more aloof to a more confidential tone, that is to a more direct attempt to confront the present perplexity and needs of the audience. In any event, in contrast to these two possibilities, an entirely different effect is generated if one construes the verbs as expressive of future actions. For then one would be inclined to perceive in the violent verbal images projected expressions of a divine fury fused by the despairing presentiment that the Israelites in exile harvested no hope from earlier acts of power, and were needful of a new display of might to make the oracles of redemption believable.

This threefold verbal ambiguity in Isaiah 50:2–3 concerning the perceived availability or viability of divine power, will not be easily unknotted. The key to its resolution may, in fact, be altogether irretrievable. And yet it is precisely in the

rhetorical intersection of this ambiguity that the modern
reader can experience an ironic correlative to the hesitations
and confusions of the original audience, to whom God "came"
and "called" His unheeded words of redemption.

Nevertheless, the memory of former times did live on in the
thoughts of Judeans yet in exile, as is reflected in the following
prayer:

> I will recount the gracious acts of YHWH,
>   even the awesome deeds of YHWH,
> For all that YHWH has requited us,
>   His great beneficence to the house of Israel,
> Which He has requited them by His love,
>   and the multitude of his faithfulness.
>
> He said: "Indeed, they are My people,
>   sons who will not be false."
> So He became their deliverer in all their afflictions.
>
> There was no envoy or messenger,*
>   but He, Himself, delivered them;
> Through His love and compassion He redeemed them,
>   He shouldered and carried them through all the days gone by.
>
> But they rebelled and grieved His holy spirit,
>   so that He became their enemy;
> And Himself fought against them.
>
> Then they recalled the days gone by,
>   Him who drew up [*mosheh*] His people:**
> "O where is He who brought them up from the sea [*yam*].
>   with the leader of His flock?
> And where is He who put in its midst
>   His holy spirit,
> Who made His awesome might
>   march at the right of Moses,
> Clearing the sea [*yam*] before them,
>   to establish for Himself a name forever;
> Who made them march through the deep *(tehomot)*,
>   Unfaltering, like a horse in the wilderness,

---

*Following many moderns the first word of v.9, "their afflictions," is
transposed to the end of v.8. The noun *tzar* is vocalized *tzir*, "envoy," following
the Septuagint version and verse parallelism.

**This reading takes God as subject with a pun on the name Moses *(Mosheh)*
and his folk etymology in Exodus 2:10. Alternatively, it may be construed:
"Moses (and) his people." Both views are mentioned by Ibn Ezra.

> Like an animal which descends to the vale,
>> the spirit of YHWH moved them on.
> So did you surely lead Your people,
>> to establish for Yourself an awesome name."

> "O look down from the heavens and see,
>> from Your holy and awesome shrine.
> Where is Your zeal and strength,
>> for they are withheld from me.
> For surely You are our father;
>> Abraham does not know us, and Israel does not acknowledge us;
> You, YHWH, are our father,
>> our redeemer whose name is forever.
> Why, YHWH, do You have us swerve from Your ways,
>> that our hearts be dulled to Your fearsome presence?
> Return for the sake of Your servants,
>> the tribes of Your inheritance.
> For they have possessed Your holy people for grief,
>> our enemies have trodden Your sanctuary.
> We have long been as ones You do not rule,
>> and over whom Your name is not called.
> O that You would rip the heavens and descend,
>> mountains would melt at Your presence!" (Isaiah 63:7-19)

From the lonely silence of the exile, the prophet gives voice to the prayer of his people who, for a time, were devoid of God's presence. Isaiah speaks words of memory and hope. God is in His holy shrine; this the speaker knows. But His presence is not felt. YHWH is addressed as a God of power. But where is His power now? Why do His people languish in exile, that their hearts be dulled to His presence when it comes? God's absence, as it were, hardens the very heart of those He will want to save. Why? Surely they are not the ancient Egyptians whose hearts He once hardened to manifest His glory. Surely they are His people. Where are You, then? asks the prophet. Where are You who performed wonders for Your people Israel?

This cry discloses a paradox of Israelite prayer. The same prayer which requests divine action at once reminds God of His former deeds, and so gives the people strength in their abyss of historical despair. The exodus is the major event remembered here: God brought Israel up *(mosheh)* from the sea by His servant Moses *(Mosheh)*, and led them through the deep *(tehomot)* with His holy spirit. The intent of the prayer is to recall God to the proven power of His ways, to arouse Him to His historical compassion and concern.

As the prayer reaches its conclusion, the tone becomes one of resolve, even defiance. There is an aggressiveness, even a new strength to the concluding words. On the surface nothing has changed. God is still silent and the people are still in exile. But the very formulation and recitation of this prayer has brought about an inner transformation. Recollection of the ancient exodus from Egypt serves the speaker as a hedge against despair and a catalyst towards renewed hope.

The simultaneous capacity of the exodus paradigm to elicit memory and expectation, recollection and anticipation, discloses once again its deep embeddedness as a fundamental structure of the biblical historical imagination. But it further discloses just what is so variously and diffusely indicated elsewhere in the Bible; namely, that the events of history are prismatic openings to the transhistorical. Indeed, the very capacity of a historical event to generate future expectation is dependent on the transfiguration of that event by the theological intuition that in it and through it the once and future power of the Lord of history is revealed. Without such a symbolic transformation, the exodus would never have given birth to hope.

Epilogue

"Interpretations come and go," said Martin Buber, "but the text remains throughout." And yet we must equally stress that the text remains precisely because of the comings and goings of interpretations. It is for this reason that everything depends on how we read; on how we enter the magic circle of a text's meanings; on how we smuggle ourselves into its words, and allow the texture of a text to weave its web around us.

Miqra, the Hebrew word for Bible, properly means "calling out." And what calls out from a text, what beckons and addresses a reader-hearer, if not its words? In a daring and remarkable comment, Rabbi Israel Ba'al Shem Tov reinterpreted the divine command "come...into the ark [*tevah*]," spoken to Noah in Genesis 7:1, as "come...into the word [*tevah*]." This comment is of suggestive significance for the hermeneutical task which we face ever and again. For guided by it, the reader of the Bible will confront the repeated or key words and themes of a biblical text, and so enter that text on its own terms. Whether these particular words or themes will remain the most significant ones for purposes of interpretation can never be known in advance. Nor can one know in advance what literary forms and structures will emerge to organize our analytic judgments. *Miqra* is thus a "calling out" to follow the lead of a text's words, themes and structures.

Miqra is also a "calling out" and revelation of the self-contained world of a text, through its particular combination of words and rhythms and structures. This is not to deny that a text may also attest to an experiential or historical reality external to it. It is rather to stress the fact that a text constitutes a self-referential world of meaning, that it is the representation of a nontextual reality in new—literary—terms. One may nevertheless hope that in and through the uniquely literary reality of a text the roots of such a nontextual reality may be revealed. At such a moment, at least with respect to the Bible, it is not only a text or an external world but God Himself who is revealed.

Miqra thus reflects, in its deepest sense, the "calling out" of God—from beyond the treasure house of human language;

from the hidden depths of *ruah*, of "spirit" or "breath," which precedes speech and animates all the forms and substances of this world. *Miqra*, the humanized and verbal record of encounters with the divine presence, is thus transcended by God. We know this, of course, or should know it. For even as the sounds and words of speech are separated by silences and breaths, so are the letters and words of texts separated by spaces and silences. The silences and breaths of speech remind us of the limitations of language, and of its fateful boldness in attempting to adjust the polyvalence of creation to the syntax and needs of mortal creatures. Correspondingly, the spaces and silences of texts remind us of the risks of interpretation— but also of its most profound hope: to find in a world of words a disclosure of the mystery of creation.

Notes

Introduction

1. Cf. *The Collected Dialogues of Plato*, ed. E. Hamilton and H. Cairns (Princeton Univ. Press, Princeton: 1964), *Phaedrus*: 275c-d.

2. For the notion "world of a text," see P. Ricouer, "The Model of the Text: Meaningful Action Considered as a Text," *Social Research* 38 (1971), pp. 535, 543, 557-58.

3. This has been discussed by S. Fish, "Literature in the Reader: Affective Stylistics, *New Literary History* 2 (1970), pp. 123-62, and W. Iser, "Indeterminacy and the Reader's Response," *Aspects of Narrative*, ed. J. H. Miller (Columbia Univ. Press, N.Y.: 1971), pp. 1-45.

4. *On Judaism* (Schocken, N.Y.: 1967), p. 172 (from: "Herut: On Youth and Religion").

Chapter 1

1. M. Eliade has devoted much attention to myths of origin; see, *e.g.*, *Myth and Reality* (Harper & Row, N.Y.: 1963), chap. 2-3. Note, also, C. Long, *Alpha; The Myths of Creation* (G. Braziller, N.Y.: 1963). A standard anthology of ancient Near Eastern creation and combat myths is J. Pritchard, *Ancient Near Eastern Texts* (Princeton Univ. Press, Princeton: 1955²), pp. 3-12, 37-44, 60-72, 99-106, 129-42; and (1969³), pp. 501-3, 517-18.

2. *Werke*, Vol. III (Wissenschaftliche Buchgesellschaft, Darmstadt: 1953), p. 392.

3. S. G. F. Brandon addresses the "propaganda" issue of many creation texts in *Creation Legends of the Ancient Near East* (Hodder & Stoughton, London: 1963).

4. K. Burke has made the helpful observation that Genesis 1 personalizes the classification of the world; see *The Rhetoric of Religion; Studies in Logology* (Beacon Press, Boston: 1961), pp. 201ff.

5. A retinue of divine beings is repeatedly referred or alluded to in the opening chapters of Genesis (see 1:26; 3:22; 6:2, 4:11:7), and elsewhere in the Hebrew Bible (e.g., 1 Kings 22:19-22; Isaiah 6:6-8; Psalms 89:7-8; 104:4; Job 4:18).

6. The phrase "that it is good" does appear in the Septuagint. Naturally enough, apologetic exegeses have "accounted" for its absence in the Massoretic text (cf. *Genesis Rabba*, IV:8, and some moderns).

7. *Midrash Ha-Gadol*, Genesis (Mosad Ha-Rav Kook, Jerusalem: 1967 n.7), pp. 54-55. Edited with notes by M. Margulies.

8. *A Commentary on the Book of Genesis*, Part I (Magnes Press, Jerusalem: 1961), pp. 16-17; trans. by I. Abrahams. I have slightly varied Cassuto's terminology to accentuate the juxtapositions.

9. Cf. A. Toeg, "Genesis 1 and the Sabbath," *Beth Miqra* 50 (1962), pp. 288-96 (Hebrew).

10. *Die Schrift und ihre Verdeutschung* (Schocken, Berlin: 1936), pp. 39ff. ("Der Mensch von heute und die judische Bibel").

11. M. Weinfeld has made similar observations in "Sabbath, Temple Building and the Enthronement of the Lord," *Beth Miqra* 69 (1977), pp. 188-93 (Hebrew). Translations of the Mesopotamian and Canaanite texts can be found in Pritchard, *op. cit.*, pp. 61, 68, 131, 133-35.

12. The impact of ancient Canaanite mythology on biblical (and later Rabbinic) literature has been discussed by U. Cassuto, "The Israelite Epic," *Biblical and Oriental Studies* II (Magnes Press, Jerusalem: 1975), pp. 69-109; trans. by I. Abrahams.

13. Cassuto in his above-noted commentary, suggested that the Bible is here sounding "a protest, as it were, against concepts that were current among Gentiles, and to a certain extent even among the Israelites." (p. 49).

Chapter 2

1. He deals with the problem of the two distinct depictions of man's creation in Genesis 1-2 in *On the Account of the World's Creation*, trans. by F. Colsen and G. Whitaker (Loeb Series; Harvard Univ. Press, 1929), par. XLVI; and in *Questions and Answers on Genesis*, trans. by R. Marcus (Loeb Series; Harvard Univ. Press, 1953), Book I, questions 4 and 8. He also raises the question of the two creations of birds and beasts, *ibid.*, question 19.

2. See M. Eliade, *Patterns in Comparative Religion* (Meridian Books, N.Y.: 1963), pp. 374-79, and A. Wensinck, *The Ideas of the Western Semites Concerning the Navel of the Earth* (Amsterdam, 1916). W. Garte has dealt with preliterary manifestations, in "Kosmische Vorstellungen im Bilde prahistorischer Zeit...," *Anthropos* 9 (1915), pp. 956-79.

3. Cassuto, in his commentary, fully delineates the differences between the Torah and prophetic passages (pp. 74-82; esp. 76-77, on the "mountain").

4. Cf. M. Buber, *Good and Evil* (Scribners, N.Y.: 1952), pp. 73-76 ("Tree of Knowledge").

5. It should not be overlooked that the serpent is a polyvalent symbol for sexuality, knowledge, and immortality. For a broadly based introduction to this image, see J. L. Henderson, *The Wisdom of the Serpent; the Myths of Death, Rebirth, and Resurrection* (G. Braziller, N.Y.: 1963).

6. P. Ricouer, *Symbolism of Evil* (Harper & Row, N.Y.: 1967), pp. 257-59 has similarly underscored the bivalent dimension to the serpent theme in Genesis 3.

7. This is the first part of a more extensive denial found in Targum Ps. Jonathan and the so-called Fragmentary Targum (*Das Fragmentanthargum*, ed. C. Ginsburg [Calvary & Co., Berlin: 1899]) on Genesis 4:8.

8. The phrase is grammatically problematic and syntactically elliptical. A review of its many problems, with possible solutions, can be found in G. Castellino, "Genesis IV 7, "*Vetus Testamentum* 10 (1960), pp. 402-5. I have translated *se'et:* "you can bear it," so as to pick up the verbal contrast with "my misdeed is too much to bear *(minnso')*" later on.

9. Cassuto notes several examples (pp. 212, 218, 225, 228); but he sees these repetitions more in the nature "of the influence exerted by epic style on narrative prose" (p. 212) than as a deliberate intertextual feature serving to occasion the concordance of Genesis 3 and 4:1-16 in the reader's mind.

10. See the edition by W.G. Lambert and A.R. Millard, *Atra-Hasis; The Babylonian Story of the Flood* (Oxford Univ. Press, Oxford: 1969). The schema of this text is: the creation of mankind; its early development and proliferation; and the employment of a flood to curtail human expansion (after two abortive attempts by the gods), from whose deluge a favored hero is saved.

11. Cassuto argued that 6:1-4 is a protest against the notion that the progeny of a union between gods and humans were immortal; see "The Episode of the Sons of God and the Daughters of Mankind (Gen. IV 1-4)," *Biblical and Oriental Studies* I (Magnes Press, Jerusalem: 1975), pp. 17-28. But his argument is forced.

12. See *Enuma elish* VI:84-92, Pritchard, *op.cit.,* p. 69.

13. See S. Kramer, "The 'Babel of Tongues': A Sumerian Version," *Journal of the American Oriental Society* 88 (1968), pp. 108-11.

14. *Die Schrift...,* pp. 214-17 ("Leitwortstil in der Erzahlung des Pentateuchs").

15. For Raddai's schema, see "Chiasm in the Biblical Narrative," *Beth Miqra* 20-21 (1964), p. 68 (Hebrew).

16. Cf. F. Steele, "The University Museum Esarhaddon Prism," *Journal of the American Oriental Society* 71 (1951), p. 7, where, in reference to the shrine of Assur, called "the house of the Great Mountain," the King states: "above to heaven I made high its top." And the later King Nabopolassar refers to a temple whose "top reached up like a mountain"; see S. Langdon, *Neubabylonische Königsinschriften* (J. Hinrichs, Leipzig: 1911), Nabopolassar: I, i, 38.

17. The use of *shem,* "name," parallel to "tower" (or ziggurat), may actually be a pun on an Akkadian expression used with regard to an inscribed monument; cf. W. F. Albright, *Yahweh and the Gods of Canaan* (Doubleday & Co., N.Y.: 1968), p. 100, and n.123.

18. The inversion *LBN/NBL* has also been observed by J.P. Fokkelman, *Narrative Art in Genesis* (Van Gorcum, Assen/Amsterdam: 1975), pp. 15-16.

Chapter 3

1. See M. Eliade, "Cosmogonic Myth and 'Sacred History,'" *The Quest; History and Meaning in Religion* (Univ. of Chicago Press, Chicago: 1969), chap. 5.

2. For an essay on biblical genealogies and their structural patterns, with specific emphasis on the Jacob Cycle, see K. Andriolo, "A Structural Analysis of Genealogy and World View in the Old Testament," *American Anthropologist* 75 (1973), pp. 1657-1669.

3. For the foregoing literature, see: Wolf, *Prolegommena ad Homerum*, 1795, ed. I. Bekker (Berlin: 1872); Wilamowitz, *Homerische Untersuchungen* (Berlin: 1884); Parry, *L'Epithete traditionelle dans Homère* (Paris: 1928), and *Les Formules et la Metrique d'Homere* (Paris: 1928).

4. *The Singer of Tales* (Harvard Univ. Press, Cambridge: 1960); cf. *Idem.* "Composition by Theme in Homer and Southslavic Epos," *Transactions of the American Philological Assn.* 82 (1951), pp. 71-80, and, in the same collection, J. Notopoulos, "Continuity and Interconnection in Homeric Oral Composition," pp. 81-101.

5. "The Last Book of the 'Iliad,'" *Journal of Hellenic Studies* 52 (1932), pp. 264-96.

6. *Homer and the Heroic Tradition* (Harvard Univ. Press, Cambridge: 1958), esp. chap. 11.

7. In his 1909 essay, "Epic Laws of Folk Narrative," translated and reprinted in A. Dundes, ed., *The Study of Folklore* (Prentice-Hall, Englewood Cliffs, N.J.: 1965), pp. 129-41.

8. The significance of the idols is clear; but whether the idols represent inheritance rights is a moot point. See M. Greenberg's "Another Look at Rachel's Theft of the Teraphim," *Journal of Biblical Literature* 81 (1962), pp. 239-48.

9. Like this description, Mesopotamian temple-towers reach "above to heaven" and descend "below on earth"; cf. Steele, *op.cit.*

10. *What Remains of the Old Testament* (London, 1928), pp. 150-86 ("Jacob").

11. Cf. A. Dundes, "From Emic to Etic Units in the Structural Study of Folktales," *Journal of American Folklore* 75 (1962), pp. 95-105.

12. *Morphology of the Folktale*, published by the *International Journal of American Linguistics* 24 (1958), translated by L. Scot. Propp completed his work in 1928.

13. R. Culley, *Studies in the Structure of Hebrew Narrative* (Fortress Press, Philadelphia: 1976), has given many biblical examples of set patterns repeated with variations.

14. This was the basis of the critique of Propp by C. Levi-Strauss, "L'analyse morphologique de contes russes," *International Journal of Slavic Linguistics and Poetics* 3 (1960), pp. 122–49.

15. This chapter is essentially a reworking of my "Composition and Structure in the Jacob Cycle (Gen. 25:19–35:22)," *Journal of Jewish Studies* 26 (1975), pp. 15–38. I have not sought to integrate it with the views simultaneously presented in J.P. Fokkelman, *Narrative Art in Genesis* (Van Gorcum, Assen/Amsterdam:1975), chap. 3.

Chapter 4

1. See Buber's reflections in *Moses; the Revelation and the Covenant* (Harper & Row, N.Y.: 1958), pp. 13-19 ("Saga and History").

2. A somewhat different breakdown of this important literary structure may be found in N. Habel, "The Form and Sign of the Call Narratives," *Zeitschrift für die alttestamentliche Wissenschaft* 77 (1965), pp. 297-323. "Signs" do not seem to be a fixed component in the prophetic commissions.

3. Cf. Shelley's remark in "A Defense of Poetry," *The Portable Romantic Reader*, H. E. Hugo, ed. (Viking Press, N.Y.: 1957), p. 536.

4. On this literary structure and its redaction, note Cassuto, *Commentary on Exodus* (Magnes Press, Jerusalem: 1967), p. 96, trans. by I. Abrahams; S. Loewenstamm, *The Tradition of the Exodus in its Development* (Magnes Press, Jerusalem: 1965), pp. 34-42 (Hebrew); and M. Greenberg, "The Redaction of the Plague Narrative in Exodus," *The Ancient Near East*, ed. H. Goedicke (Johns Hopkins Univ. Press, Baltimore: 1971), pp. 243-52.

5. See Talmon's *"Hatan-Damim," Eretz Israel* 3 (1954), pp. 93–96 (Hebrew). For the problematics of the passage, cf. Childs, *The Book of Exodus* (Westminster, Phila.: 1974), pp. 92, 95-102.

6. Cf. Buber, *op.cit.*, pp. 58-59.

7. Compare the discussion in Childs, *op.cit.*, pp. 93-95.

8. *Understanding Exodus* (Behrman House, N.Y.: 1969), pp. 130-36.

9. Among medieval commentators, this triadic structure was also noted by Rashbam (at Exodus 7:26) and Bahya (at Exodus 10:11).

Chapter 5

1. Other question and answer instructional patterns appear in the Bible (Exodus 13:8, 14 and Joshua 4:6), and may have originally functioned in a cultic context; so J. A. Soggin, "Kult-ätiologische Sagen und Katechese in Hexateuch," *Vetus Testamentum* 10 (1960), pp. 341-47.

2. I am indebted to E. Rosenstock-Heussy for the pointed neologism "distemporaries"; see his *Speech and Reality* (Argo Books, Norwich, N.H.: 1970), esp. p. 33 and references ("In Defense of the Grammatical Method").

3. For the scholarly discussion on this chapter, see Childs, *op.cit.*, chap. 10. Childs correctly emphasizes (pp. 251-52) that the nexus between the exodus and the conquest need not be artificial but organic, as in Isaiah 63:11ff.; Psalms 77:15ff. Verbal links between the two parts of the hymn will be indicated in chap. 10, below.

4. The poetic use of Exodus 19:1,6 in Psalm 114:1-2 has been acutely detected by M. Weiss, *The Bible and Modern Literary Theory* (Bialik, Jerusalem: 1967), p. 181 (Hebrew).

Chapter 6

1. "Psalm XIX and the Near Eastern Sun-God Literature," *Proceedings of IV World Congress of Jewish Studies*, I (World Union of Jewish Studies, Jerusalem: 1967), pp. 171-75. For representative Hymns to the Sun, see Pritchard, *op.cit.*, pp. 367-71, 387-89.

2. *Ibid.*, p. 175.

3. Note the formulation of R. Shemuel bar Nahman in *Genesis Rabba* XXX:3: "Everywhere [the name] YHWH occurs [in Scripture there you will find] the attribute of mercy...everywhere Elohim occurs: the attribute of justice..."

Chapter 7

1. For an introduction to Jeremiah's lament-prayers and their legal structure, see S. Blank, "The Confessions of Jeremiah and the Meaning of Prayer," *Hebrew Union College Annual* 21 (1948), pp. 331-54. Blank also addressed the question why Jeremiah's private prayers were included among his public oracles, in "The Prophet as Paradigm," *Essays in Old Testament Ethics*, J. L. Crenshaw and J. T. Willes, eds. (Ktav, N.Y.: 1974), pp. 111-30.

2. The medieval commentators Rashi and Kimhi understood these verbs as bearing on Jeremiah's commission; S.D. Luzzato understood them as public proclamations whereby Jeremiah indicated that he prophesied by *force majeur*, and so hoped to evoke a corresponding sense of necessity (for repentance) in his listeners.

3. Most medieval commentators understood the shout to be about the social evils which Jeremiah witnessed; by contrast, R. Joseph Kara understood Jeremiah's shout to be about evils directed against his person.

4. See J. J. A. Clines and D. Gunn, "'You Tried to Persuade Me' and 'Violence!, Outrage' in Jer XX, 7-8," *Vetus Testamentum* 28 (1978), pp. 25-26.

5. The dimensions of the inner and the outer are varied in Jeremiah. J. Starobinski has provided a suggestive literary probe into this typology; see his "The Inside and the Outside," *The Hudson Review* 28 (1975), pp. 33-51.

6. Based on "wretched things of shame, mere bellies," Hesiod, *Theogony*, line 26.

7. For related matters, see K. Burke, "On Musicality in Verse," *The Philosophy of Literary Form* (Louisiana State Univ. Press, Baton Rouge: 1941), pp. 369–78; and also D. Hymes, "Phonological Aspects of Style: Some English Sonnets," *Style and Language*, T. Sebeok, ed. (M.I.T. Press, Cambridge: 1960), pp. 109–31.

8. Many features within this prayer correspond to the types of consonant clusters, reversals, and augmentations discussed by Burke, *op.cit.* For other alliterative patterns in Jeremiah's prayer, note: *PiTTiytaniy Va'ePPaT* (v.7); *'aTZur Be'aTZmotay* (v.9); *haGGiDu venaGGiDennu* (v.10); *NiQhah NiQmatenu* (v.10).

9. Cf. M. Bloomfield, "The Syncategorematic in Poetry: From Semantics to Syntactics," *To Honor Roman Jakobson* (Moulon, Paris: 1967), pp. 309–17; G. Hartman, "The Voice of the Shuttle: Language from the Point of View of Literature," *Beyond Formalism* (Yale Univ. Press, New Haven: 1975), pp. 337–55.

10. While Jeremiah's outcry and its transition to praise follow a pattern commonly found in biblical psalms of lament (cf. W. Baumgartner, *Die Klagedichte des Jeremiah* [BZAW 32 Geissen:1917], pp. 48–51, 63–67), these traditional factors may have helped organize Jeremiah's response to his situation. It would be folly to reduce a private prayer solely to formal constraints.

Chapter 8

1. Interpretation of this stanza is complicated by the fact that the object of "Beseech" is different from the object of "May those who love you." Different emendations have been proposed. I prefer a request with a quote, a solution which has the advantage of fitting the life setting of this Psalm and what is known of priestly invocations to pilgrims (see below).

2. Cf. the remarks of S. Spiegel, "A Prophetic Attestation of the Decalogue: Hosea 6:5," *Harvard Theological Review* 27 (1934), parts III–IV, pp. 120–39.

Chapter 9

1. See chap. 2, n.2, above.

2. On the preceding remarks, cf. P.L. Berger's consideration: "The concept of the religious motif...refers to a specific pattern or gestalt of religious experience, that can be traced in a historical development"; see "The Sociological Study of Sectarianism," *Social Research* 21 (1954), p. 477.

3. The study of biblical motifs raises questions as to their transmission and transpositions. For an early exploration, cf. H. Gross, "Motivtransposition als Überlieferungsgeschichtliches Prinzip im Alten Testament," *Sacra Pagina* 1 (1958), pp. 324–34.

4. Reflections on the symbol of the sacred center, and the need for a

special methodology, are offered by M. Eliade, "Psychologie et histoire des religions—A propos du symbolisme du 'centre,'" *Eranos-Jahrbuch* 19 (1950), pp. 247-82.

5. See chap. 2, n. 3, above; and H. May, "The King in the Garden of Eden: A Study of Ezekiel 28:12-19," *Israel's Prophetic Heritage*, B. Anderson and W. Harrelson, eds. (Harper & Row, N.Y.: 1962), pp. 166-76. For a wide-ranging treatment, see G. Widengren, *The King and the Tree of Life in Ancient Near Eastern Religion* (Uppsala Universitets Arsskrift IV; Lundequistska, Uppsala:1951).

6. For the correspondence between heavenly and earthly shrines from a "history of religions" perspective, see M. Eliade, "Centre du Monde, Temple, Maison," *Le Symbolisme Cosmique des Monuments Religieux*, E. Oriente, ed. (Rome: 1957), pp. 57-82; for the theme in classical Jewish sources, see V. Aptowitzer, "The Cosmic Temple according to Rabbinic Sources," *Tarbiz* 31 (1930-31), pp. 137-53, 257-87 (Hebrew).

7. Cf. simply, M. Eliade, *Patterns in Comparative Religion*, pp. 231-33 (and bibliography, p. 238). On some rabbinic traditions see R. Patai, *Man and Temple; In Ancient Jewish Myth and Ritual* (Nelson & Sons, London: 1947), pp. 55-59, 85; and see chap. 3 generally on the "Temple and Creation Myths" in this literature.

8. Consonantal *'ry'l* (Ariel) in Isaiah 29:1 is also found in Ezekiel 43:15-16, and most probably reflects Akkadian *arallu*, meaning both "mountain of the gods" and "underworld."

9. Cf. Patai, *op.cit.* For the biblical traditions, and their ancient Near Eastern analogues, see the discussion following.

10. See W. F. Albright, *Archeology and the Religion of Israel* (Doubleday-Anchor, N.Y.: 1969[5]), pp. 146-47. And cf. n.8, above.

11. Cf. the Akkadian expression *irat ersitti/kigalle*, "bosom of the earth" or "bosom of the underworld"; noted by Albright, *op.cit.* Examples of this expression may be found in Langdon, *op.cit.*, in the inscriptions of Nabopolassar (I, i, 36) and NebuKhadnezzar (I, ii, 31; IV; 29-30; VI, ii, 1-2; XII, ii, 23), and see chap.3, n.9, above.

12. Patai, *op.cit.*, pp. 86-87; and see H. Frankfort, *The Art and Architecture of the Ancient Orient* (Penguin, Hammondsworth: 1954), p. 63 and Pl. 72.

13. Cf. M. Eliade's suggestive essay, "Nostalgia for Paradise in the Primitive Traditions," *Myths, Dreams, and Mysteries* (Harper Torchbook, N.Y.: 1967), pp. 59-72. For the transformation of this longing into utopian fantasy and energy, see F. &. F. Manuel, "Sketch for a Natural History of Paradise," *Daedalus*, Winter 1972, pp. 83-128.

Chapter 10

1. A related, but different, aspect of the exodus motif is the way it affected historical narratives, and was itself affected by legal considerations; see D. Daube, *The Exodus Pattern in the Bible* (Faber & Faber, London: 1963).

2. Cf. the remarks made and literature adduced in chap. 5 above. And see the discussion below.

3. On the relationship between cosmogony and eschatology, see M. Eliade, *Myth and Reality*, chap. 4.

4. This *topos* in Canaanite and biblical literature has been reviewed by C. H. Gordon, "Leviathan: Symbol of Evil," *Biblical Motifs; Origins and Transformations*, A. Altmann, ed. Brandeis Univ. Texts and Studies III (Harvard Univ. Press, Cambridge: 1966), pp. 1-9.

5. This link between Exodus 15 and Canaanite myth is also discussed by F. Cross, *Canaanite Myth and Hebrew Epic* (Harvard Univ. Press, Cambridge: 1973), chap. 6.

6. This structure further reinforces our contention that the hymn is a unified composition; see chap. 5, n.3, and the verbal links between the two parts of the hymn noted earlier in this chapter.

7. Menes, "Temple und Synagogue," *Zeitschrift für die alttesamentliche Wissenschaft* 50 (1932), pp. 272-73; Greenberg, "Ezekiel 20 and the Spiritual Exile," *'Oz Le-David*, Festschrift Ben Gurion (Kiryat Sepher, Jerusalem: 1964), p. 440 (Hebrew).

8. An earlier treatment of the "Exodus Typology in Second Isaiah," was made by B. Anderson, in *Israel's Prophetic Heritage*, B. Anderson and W. Harrelson, eds. (New York, 1962), pp. 177-95. Some of his suggestions are dubious; and he has overlooked other features treated below.

9. See n.3, above, regarding the thematic link between cosmogony and eschatology.

10. Among recent translations, *The New English Bible* (1971) construes the verbs in the past tense, whereas the *Jerusalem Bible* (1966) and the New Jewish Publication Society *Isaiah* (1973) construe them as reflecting present activity or capacity.

Index: "Text and Texture"